The Golden Years of Merseybeat

Acknowledgements

I would like to thank everybody for their interviews and help with photographs for this book. Thanks also go to my wife Irene, Carla, Lee, Leanne and grandchildren Laura, Olivia and Thomas Lee for their continuing support. I would also like to say a big thankyou to Harry Prytherch for all his help. Thank you to Colour Print, John Lomax, Len Garry, John Byrne, Sam Hardy, Brian Woods, Frankie Connor, Ian Edwards, Joe Butler, Les Brade, Tony Sanders, Dave Williams, Geoff Nugent, Billy Butler, Faron, Bobby Scott, Karl Terry, Dave Kent, Ray Scragg, Tom Flude, Dave Forshaw, Stan Johnson, Denis Donafee, Alan Lucket, Mike Edwards, Dave Peacock, George Dixon, Bernie Rogers, Bill Jones, Frank Townsend, Colin Hanton, Billy Kinsley, Vera Nugent, Bernie Wenton, Allan Schroeder, Joe Bower, John Cross, Richey Prescott, Gerry Marsden, Mike Evans, Ralph Webster, Ken Dean, Kenny Johnson, Lyn Keller, Sugar Deen, Tommy Hughes, Albert Wycherley, Mel Roberts and Bob Wooler.

I would like to dedicate this book to all my family.

Published by The Bluecoat Press, Liverpool
Printed and bound in Great Britain
Book design by MARCH Graphic Design Studio, Liverpool

ISBN 1 904438 60 1

The Golden Years of Merseybeat

Eric Woolley

The Bluecoat Press

Contents

Introduction

The Official
Beatles FAN CLUB
P.O. Box No. 12,
LIVERPOOL, 1.
THIS IS TO CERTIFY THAT
....
IS AN OFFICIALLY ENROLLED MEMBER
OF THE FAN CLUB AND HAS BECOME
BEATLE PERSON NUMBER
Freda Kelly
Freda Kelly
National Secretary of The Official Beatles Fan Club

Now a major tourist attraction, Liverpool is not only renowned for its architectural splendour and seaport heritage, but also for its music, which, in its heyday in the 1960s, came to be known as the Merseybeat. Foremost amongst this emerging rush of talent were The Beatles. In his unrelenting quest to get the group signed up to a major recording company, Brian Epstein eventually saw their first record as The Beatles, *Love Me Do,* released on 11 October 1962, on the Parlophone label, opening the door to seventeen number one hits for the group over the coming years. At the same time, many of the top recording labels vied with each other to sign up other groups and artists from the overwhelming array of talent that this Mersey sound had to offer. The name Merseybeat evolved from the local music paper of the same name, that was run by a college friend of John Lennon's, Bill Harry.

At a charity jam night organised by The Merseycats Rock and Roll children's charity, I met Freda Kelly, who was The Beatles Fan Club secretary from 1963 through to 1975, having taken over from Bobbie Brown, who originally started with the fan club in 1962. Freda worked for NEMS in Whitechapel during the day and at night for The Beatles fan club, until the latter became a full time job. She also had a column in *The Disc and Music Echo* through Ray Coleman. Freda told me that she felt that The Beatles had opened up the floodgates for other talented Merseybeat groups to go on to greater things and make their mark on the contemporary music scene, although some of them were so talented that they would almost certainly have achieved success sooner or later anyway. Asked which of all the Merseybeat groups should have made a greater impact than they did, she unhesitatingly came up with The Big Three. I would agree, along with most of the other hundreds of Merseyside musicians who saw any of their exciting (and extremely loud) live performances. Having signed up for Decca, their first release was *Some Other Guy / Let True Love Begin*, in March 1963, quickly followed by, *By the Way / Cavern Stomp*, in June of the same year. Their next release came in October with *I'm With You / Peanut Butter*, then an EP – *The Big Three at the Cavern* – containing four tracks: *Some Other Guy, By The Way, Reelin' and a Rockin'* and *Zip-A-Dee-Do-Dah*. The next single didn't emerge until June 1964 – *If You Ever Change Your Mind / You've Got to Keep Her Under Hand*.

However, Merseybeat was not so much about individual brilliance, although that was there in plenty, but about a generation of ordinary kids just picking up a guitar and a set of drums and getting together to make music, in an explosion of talent which put Liverpool, and the groups which emerged from it, at the centre of the world stage.

I have selected out forty-two of the best local groups to represent this vast array of talent, groups which made a significant contribution to the Mersey Sound in the late fifties through to the sixties, from Jazz and Skiffle to Merseybeat.

Lonnie Donegan
the Leading Light of Skiffle

"… a world class performer who paved the way for British popular music as we know it today." This quote, from Lonnie's long-standing friend Mel Roberts, sums up the legendary Lonnie Donegan. Anthony James Donegan was born on 29 April 1931, in Glasgow, of Scottish / Irish parents. Influenced by New Orleans Jazz and the American Blues, Lonnie taught himself the guitar at the age of fourteen and soon found himself fronting The Tony Donegan Jazz Band and playing in the London Jazz club scene. The band was asked to be the opening act at the Royal Festival Hall, where the star of the bill was American Blues singer, Lonnie Johnson, whom Lonnie had admired for many years. The compere, on introducing The Tony Donegan Jazz Band, mistakenly announced them as The Lonnie Donegan Jazz Band. Nerves had probably got the better of him, but the name has stuck ever since.

Lonnie, a guitar and banjo player, heavily influenced by Blues and Jazz, joined The Ken Colyer Band, along with Chris Barber, who fronted the band after Ken had decided to leave over some discord concerning their musical direction. The Chris Barber Jazz Band released an album featuring Lonnie Donegan and including the song, *Rock Island Line*. The song was singled out by Decca, who released it in 1956, selling three million copies and making it a hit with fans in Britain and the United States.

Lonnie had now found a new direction, and then his career really took off with an appearance on the *Perry Como Show* and a tour of America. He then moved from Decca and signed for the PYE label, with which he released some memorable recordings. At that point, unknown to himself, Lonnie had become a guiding light to up and coming musicians, myself included, all over Britain, including new Skifflers such as John Lennon's Quarry Men, The Blue Genes Skiffle Group, The Eddie Clayton Skiffle Group, The Texans and many more. Skiffle was now beginning to compete with Jazz bands in and around Liverpool.

Skiffle Competes with Jazz

Lonnie Donegan released his version of *Rock Island Line* in 1956, which started the Skiffle boom and, by 1957, the whole country was in the grip of the Skiffle sound, but traditional Jazz could still be heard echoing from the clubs and cellars down the backstreets of Liverpool. It was a time when stars were born almost overnight, helped by television programmes like *The 6.5 Special*, which went out on Saturday nights, keeping thousands of teenagers transfixed. Produced by Jack Good, the show was broadcast at 6.05pm and was on a roll introducing up and coming new stars.

The American artists were leading the way in the music scene, with Elvis Presley and Bill Haley rocking them in the aisles. Meanwhile, the Skiffle groups in Liverpool were forming at the rate of almost one a week, borrowing their mothers' washboards and a couple of thimbles, a tea-chest and a pole with a string attached. All that was then needed was someone who could strum at least three chords on a guitar and they were away! An undercurrent of untapped Liverpool talent was simmering on a low light, waiting to burst on to the music scene. Groups such as The Swinging Blue Genes and the Raving Texans were all being influenced by shows like *Oh Boy!* which introduced stars like Marty Wilde, who took the country by storm.

Meanwhile, the Skiffle groups in Liverpool were getting a foot in the door, playing their music in the coffee houses and Jazz clubs of the city, in the late fifties, when Jazz still ruled. The Jazz audiences were gradually being won over by this new Skiffle sound, which was derived from the influences of Lonnie Donegan, Chas McDevitt and Nancy Whiskey.

A new boom was under way and Liverpool was awash with Skiffle groups, Skiffle contests and talent shows, but it was not all plain sailing, as John Lomax from The Atlantics Skiffle Group commented, "They were great times – well, maybe not all of it was great!" Getting to and from bookings was problematic, most groups relying on public transport, since few people had their own transport. John recalls his first visit to the Cavern in Mathew Street, when *The Liverpool Echo* advertised a Grand Skiffle Contest to be held at the club for the Lonnie Donegan Skiffle Trophy. It was held on the evening of Wednesday, 16 April 1958, the prize being an appearance on *The 6.5 Special* television show.

The Atlantics registered their name for the contest, but being Wallasey based, they had to make their way by bus to the ferry terminal, where they boarded the *Royal Daffodil* to cross the Mersey. Once on board, they decided to have one last rehearsal, but unfortunately, the captain did not share their taste in music and warned that if they did not stop the racket, he would have them thrown overboard! The band obediently packed away their instruments and made their way down to the lower deck to wait for the gangway to be lowered on reaching Pier Head. From there they still had a ten minute walk to the Cavern, carrying all their gear.

Once in Mathew Street, they managed to locate the small doorway halfway down on the right-hand side, then down the steps into the gloomy, sparsely-lit cellar. John described it as being like a dark tunnel, until his eyes adjusted, and then a small stage within an arch could be made out at one end, with a bar and cloakroom at the other side selling soft drinks. The club soon filled up and the air became choked with tobacco smoke, as most people in those days smoked. The stage was barely adequate to hold one group's gear, especially if they had a drum kit. The Cavern was a fire hazard, with condensation streaming down the walls and no ventilation, but the groups and their audiences still enjoyed every minute of it.

Some of the Liverpool groups stood out as being exceptionally talented. One in particular was the Remo Quartet, later becoming the Remo Four, all excellent musicians. As a guitarist myself, I must give special mention to Colin Manley, one of the most laid back but outstanding lead instrumental, Duane Eddy-style guitarists around at the time. He later joined The Swinging Blue Jeans, sadly the last group he played with before he passed away.

Just as we thought that Skiffle was here to stay, the Rock and Roll sound began to creep in to replace it, as early as 1958, and some groups even began to emulate the new sound prior to that – Chuck Berry, Little Richard and Elvis Presley providing the predominant role models.

The club proprietors were becoming aware of their audiences' preference for Rock and Roll and since it was the audiences that brought in the money, they eventually came round to booking more such groups. Tea-chest bass and acoustic guitars gradually started to be replaced by electric ones. The Quarry Men were one such hybrid Skiffle / Rock group, led by John Lennon, then an ardent Rock and Roller itching to break free from the Skiffle scene.

One superb group waiting in the wings, and already influenced by Rock and Roll, was Kingsize Taylor and the Dominoes. In Gerry Marsden's eyes, "They were the best live Rock and Roll group in Liverpool." This group of rockers should have made more of an impression in the music world than they did and it may have been their extended stay in Germany that stunted their fame. Nevertheless, they left their mark on the Merseybeat scene. Their sound can be heard on some excellent recordings on Decca and Polydor, with other releases under the name of The Shakers. Kingsize Taylor was a real power-house of a singer, something which can be appreciated on his versions of *Money, Memphis Tennesee*, and *Doctor Feel Good*. Gerry Marsden also had a good sound surfacing from the Skiffle boom, slowly gravitating towards Rock and Roll. Gerry's band seemed to have the edge on the other groups, with the addition of a piano player, Les Maguire, acquired from The Undertakers. Incidentally, The Undertakers were another force to be reckoned with, featuring some outstanding saxophone playing from Brian Jones.

The Liverpool music scene was noticeably changing and talent scouts and recording studios were keeping a close eye on the up and coming groups and singers. Theatre tour managers like Larry Parnes were also taking a keen interest in the Liverpool scene. One of the greatest talents to join the Larry Parnes stable of stars, was a young lad from the Dingle area of Liverpool, Ronnie Wycherley, who auditioned at the Essoldo Theatre in Birkenhead. Larry Parnes spotted a star in the making in Ronnie and immediately took him under his wing. He also gave him a new name and from that day onwards Billy Fury was launched as a household name. His sultry good looks and dynamic stage presence shook the country within a very short time, leaving us some memorable recordings, one of his best undoubtedly being *The Sound of Fury*. Incidentally, Larry Parnes made arrangements to audition some of the Liverpool groups who were around at the time to back Billy. The audition was held at the Wyvern Club on 10 May 1960, and guess who turned up? Of course, our old friends, The Quarry Men, under their new name, The Silver Beetles. I think, by this time, we can safely say that the Skiffle era had passed, except, perhaps, amongst the few ardent Lonnie Donegan fans. The Liverpool musicians were beginning to create their own unique sound.

The Skiffle boom was a great stepping stone for amateur musicians in and around the Liverpool area; a cheap introduction to the music world, as a washboard could be found quite easily in the late fifties, and a tea-chest bass a relatively simple instrument to make and you could often pick up a cheap acoustic guitar from one of the many of second-hand shops. If fortune was really on your side, you also had a drummer. If all else failed, there was always the all-in-one Viceroy Skiffle Board on the market, complete with drum, washboard, cowbell, tap-box, rim-shot and hooter. Although I never actually saw one being used in Liverpool, there were probably groups in London, where they were manufactured, that used them.

One of the most exciting groups to emerge from the Skiffle scene, and who were there at the start, were Rory Storm and the Hurricanes, originally called the Texans, with Alan Caldwell on lead vocals, John Byrne on guitar, Paul Murphy on guitar vocals, Jeff Truman on tea-chest bass and Reg Hales on washboard. When they became The Raving Texans, Jeff Truman decided to leave and Spud Ward stepped in on bass. The group once again changed their name to Al Storm and the Hurricanes, eventually ending up as Rory Storm and the Hurricanes. By this time,

Ringo Starr was a well established member of the group, accompanying Charles O'Brien on guitar, Wally Eymond on bass, John Byrne on guitar and Rory Storm on lead vocals. Incidentally, in 1957 Paul Murphy and John Byrne recorded two songs on an acetate record at Percy Phillips recording studio in Kensington, Liverpool: *Butterfly*, by Charlie Gracie, which reached number twelve in the charts in 1957, and *She's Got It*, which reached number fifteen in the British charts for Little Richard, also in 1957. Gibson Kemp was the replacement drummer with the Hurricanes when Ringo left the group in August 1962 to join The Beatles, who also started their career as a Skiffle group – The Quarry Men.

Goodbye to Skiffle
Merseybeat is Coming

The Cavern Club became almost a shrine to some Merseyside musicians; a popular place to congregate and watch other groups and maybe even steal a song or two. It was around mid-summer 1960 when one of the German club owners in Hamburg started to attract British groups to play in the red light district of St Pauli. One of the first Liverpool groups to venture over there was Derry and the Seniors. Derry Wilkie was the front man, with a dynamic voice, backed up by Howie Casey on saxophone. Also in the line-up was Brian Griffiths on lead guitar. Brian later joined one of Liverpool's top groups, The Big Three. The Seniors played in the style of Fats Domino and Little Richard, creating a rip-roaring Rock and Roll sound.

The group went to Germany to work for Bruno Koshmider, and with the aid of Allan Williams, they played at the Kaiserkeller. Koshmider was impressed with The Seniors and asked Allan to send out another Liverpool group to play at the Indra Club, in St Pauli. Allan Williams was, by this time, looking after our old friends The Silver Beetles, who were having great difficulty in obtaining a steady drummer and he offered them the job on the understanding that they found themselves one. The group auditioned Pete Best, who not only had his own drum kit, but was also available to go to Germany. Although The Seniors did not think it a good move sending The Silver Beetles out, Allan went ahead with the deal and sent them anyway.

Meanwhile, back in Liverpool, the groups were improving all the time, finding more and more clubs to play in, such as The Orrell Park Ballroom, New Brighton Tower Ballroom and The Iron Door, to name but a few. Bob Wooler was starting to get a lot of recognition around Liverpool as a disc jockey and was also instrumental in finding names for some of the groups. The up and coming musicians formed groups like Cass and the Casanovas, a raunchy band who ended up as The Big Three, leaving us an excellent legacy in the form of a live EP, *At the Cavern*, on Decca. Another excellent Liverpool group, also captured on vinyl, was Lee Curtis and the All Stars, a group in which Pete Best ended up later in his career, leaving behind some great singles like *Let's Stomp, What About Me, Ecstasy* and *Little Girl.*

I considered The Dennisons to be in a class of their own and they were also generous in their encouragement of other groups. Another great sound came from Johnny Sandon and the Searchers, fronted by Johnny for a while, until he joined The Remo Four, who released very good versions of *Magic Potion* and *Lies*. They backed various artists such as Tommy Quickly, but also recorded in their own right, including an excellent version of Duane Eddie's *Peter Gunn,* in which Colin Manley was at his best.

Liverpool was building up a spectacular array of groups, some influenced by Rhythm and Blues and others by Rock and Roll. Hamburg's magnetism was still strong, attracting more and more groups to the nightclubs of the red light district. Many of those who made the journey had no idea what they were getting themselves into – long hours on stage, sleazy accommodation, not to mention feuding nightclub owners and their henchmen. However, it didn't bother groups like Kingsize Taylor and the Dominoes, because Teddy Taylor weighed twenty stone and was six foot five, and therefore big enough to cope with it. The money was reasonable, so they decided to base themselves in Germany for a while, along with Ian and the Zodiacs, another talented group from Liverpool who became firm favourites in Germany. Judged by his manager to be one of the best vocalists in Liverpool, Ian later joined another great Merseybeat group,

The Fourmost (originally The Four Jays), who were a close, a cappella-style harmony group, who sadly disbanded, but only after recording a great LP on Parlophone entitled *First and Fourmost*.

Oddly enough, there were very few female vocalists to emerge from this great explosion of Merseyside talent. One of the few was Beryl Marsden, who sang at the Cavern and was backed by many of the top Liverpool groups. She went on to greater things and is now well known on the continent. Cilla Black started out working at the Cavern and was backed by some great groups such as Kingsize Taylor and the Dominoes and even The Beatles. The Vernons Girls made a slight impact at one time, as did The Liver Birds.

The Beatles were back home recovering from their eye-opening trip to Germany, an experience that either made or broke a group, as their first trip nearly did for The Beatles. However, they had gained plenty of experience through constant playing, as well as expanding their repertoire. The Beatles then made their second trip to Hamburg, this time to play the Top Ten Club.

Liverpool saw the introduction of a new music magazine, Merseybeat, which was introduced by Bill Harry on 5 July 1961 and gave the Liverpool groups a lot of coverage, as it was distributed around the music shops. One shop in particular was NEMS, which had a record department run by Brian Epstein, who, of course, went on to manage The Beatles. Brian saw a chance to break into music management and the recording side of the business, through the talent he recognised in the group. He detected the magnetic effect they had on their audiences and although they still had some rough edges to iron out, he was prepared to take on the task and help them break into the recording media. Many others, such as Cilla Black, Gerry Marsden and the Pacemakers and Billy J Kramer and the Dakotas were to follow.

A Selection of Groups Who Represented the Mersey Sound

I have featured forty-two local groups to represent the vast array of talent which contributed to the Mersey Sound in the late fifties, right through to the end of the sixties.

The Atlantics

The Atlantics Skiffle Group was an idea of John Lomax's that became reality. In 1957, John was a piano repairer by trade, but also an accomplished pianist. He bought himself a second-hand guitar and got together with his friends Ron Harrison and Ron Higginson, the latter having just acquired a Framus guitar. The three set about starting up a Skiffle group. It was decided that Ron Higginson would take on guitar and vocals, John would take on guitar and Ron Harrison would go on tea-chest bass. The three joined forces and made the tea-chest bass for Ron to play. Rehearsals started and they began styling themselves on Lonnie Donegan's Skiffle group. They used every spare moment to learn new songs, and brush up on their guitar chords with the help of John Lomax. They then decided it was time to bring in a drummer, so an advertisement was put in the paper and was answered by Tony Cavanagh, who fitted well into the group. They rehearsed with their new drummer and after mastering fifty or so songs, decided it was time to hit the clubs and dance halls.

Their first booking was at the Manganese-Bronze Club, Wallasey. Their practising had paid off, The Atlantics went from strength to strength and Ron was able to afford a second-hand double bass. The Atlantics made a few appearances at the club and on one of these occasions they were approached by the secretary of the Unicorn Jazz Club, in Duke Street. The group were booked to play for six months, playing two or three nights a week alongside many famous names of the day.

The Atlantics then had a change in their line-up when Tony left the group and they acquired a new drummer, Alan Wharton, who also took on the tedious task of securing bookings. On one occasion he talked the lads into hiring the New Brighton Tower Ballroom for a Skiffle and Jazz revival night, along with The Bill Gregson Band and three other groups. The posters and tickets were printed and the show went ahead, but they only just broke even. However, this venture did open up some doors for the group, as they were booked to play on board the *Royal Iris* for the Riverboat Shuffle.

For many groups around that time, the line-up tended to change every few months or so and The Atlantics were no exception, with Alan Wharton soon deciding it was time to move on and Ken Hardy brought into the group, which was good because he was slightly older and more experienced than the rest of the lads. The group also acquired a new lead singer, Ken 'Mr Music' Hughes, when Ron Higginson got married and moved down South. The group then had the offer of work in Australia, as there was a shortage of groups out there, but declined the offer. The bass player Ron finally got married and also moved away, to North Wales.

The group carried on playing together until their bookings petered out and finally disbanded in 1963. The final line-up was, John Lomax on guitar, Ron Harrison on bass, Ken Hughes on guitar / vocals and Ken Hardy on drums. Sadly, Ron Higginson passed away in 1998 and John Lomax is now a member of the Cheshire Cats, a charity that raises money for children, and spends a lot of his time recording the original Merseybeat groups, who put on shows for charity. John revived the Atlantics in 1993, restoring three out of the four of the original members.

The Almost Young

A Kirkby based group, which started out in late 1967, The Almost Young followed in the footsteps of The Drifters, The Four Tops and The Temptations, in terms of style. The line-up was Chris Dwyer – who had an instinctive feel for Soul music – on lead vocals, Tommy Bradley on drums, Charlie Henry on lead guitar, John Mckeown on bass and Mike Edwards on rhythm guitar / vocals. The Almost Young played places like the Litherland Town Hall, as well as lots of local youth dances. I first saw them perform at Litherland while I was still guitarist with Tyme and Motion, and I was impressed by the way the audience instantly warmed to them, demonstrating their potential to become a top recording group. However, they disbanded around the same time that Tyme and Motion were beginning to fall apart. Not long afterwards, Bobby Milne and Eric Woolley from Tyme and Motion, joined The Almost Young, and the band auditioned for *Opportunity Knocks*, but nothing came of it. The opportunity arose to travel and work abroad for three months, with one month in Germany and two in Turkey, entertaining the American forces. The trip was organised by Micky Heyes. We all gave up our day jobs and travelled to Neckersone in Germany, on 28 October 1969, with the chance of an optional nine month contract.

We set off in our old Thames van, but about three quarters of the way through Germany it broke down on the autobahn and had to be towed to the nearest garage. We then had to transfer all our equipment by taxi to the train station to get to the camp. We were later picked up in army lorries and taken to our hotel, turning the whole episode into quite an experience. While we were in Germany we were told we could not proceed to Turkey, due to the troubles there, so we stayed on in Germany instead. When we eventually arrived back in Liverpool, the long hours playing six nights a week were manifested in how tight we were as a group. The show that remains most vivid in my memory, was when we were support group to Bob and Earl on their Harlem Shuffle Tour.

The final line-up of The Almost Young, when they disbanded in the early 1970s, was Chris Dwyer, John McKeown, Mike Edwards, Bobby Milne and Eric Woolley

The Black Knights

Allan Schroeder, the drummer with the Black Knights, was brought up in Wirral, and at the age of eleven, moved to Gorsedale Secondary Modern School in Wallasey. Brian Jones (saxophone) also attended Gorsedale School, and later joined one of Liverpool's top Rock and Roll groups, The Undertakers, who made a name for themselves in the British charts under the PYE label. Another well known musician, Les Maguire, was also a pupil. It was probably no coincidence that all three of them were members of the school brass band. Les eventually joined Gerry Marsden and the Pacemakers as the keyboard player, with three successive number ones in the charts under the management of Brian Epstein. Allan's interest in music stems from his school band days, where he was second trombonist.

Allan Schroeder joined the Black Knights around the end of 1961. It all started at a place called the Witches' Cauldron, with Kenny Griffiths on vocals / lead guitar, Bill Kenny on bass guitar / vocals and Allan on drums. Norman Hurst, the group's manager, came round to Allan's house to inform them that there was an audition for a new film, *Ferry Cross the Mersey,* starring Gerry Marsden. The group went over to Liverpool to meet Gerry Marsden's manager, Les Hurst, at the Adelphi Hotel. He explained that, for the purposes of the film, they were looking for a wild group to compete against Gerry Marsden in a talent competition. The group passed the audition and spent two or three days at the Locarno Ballroom in Liverpool rehearsing and filming. The group then recorded a single on the Columbia label (DB 7443) *I Got a Woman / Angel of Love,* written by Kenny Griffiths. They also featured on the American LP *Ferry Cross the Mersey.*

Like most of the Merseyside groups around that time, Hamburg still held a great appeal. The Black Knights found themselves with a contract in June 1965, for six weeks, acquired through their manager Norman Hurst as a result of their recording of *I Got a Woman* and their film appearance. They headed off to the Star Club but things did not run as smoothly as they would have liked. On the way through the French customs in Boulogne, they had their Selmer Amplifiers impounded (they were sponsored by Selmer), so had to use the house equipment, or that of the other groups. They were offered a further engagement in Germany on the understanding that they had the use of the house equipment, but on arrival they were informed that there was no equipment available, which was a big disappointment for the group. After their six-week gig at the Star Club, they made their way back to Boulogne to collect their equipment on the return journey to England. The Black Knights stayed together until August 1965. Allan has since rekindled the band but with an alternative line-up. They do a lot of work for charity.

The Buzz Brothers

Brothers Bobby, Willie and Bernie Wenton formed the line-up, backed by numerous bands. Here in the photograph, they make up Black Magic. On the back row, from left to right, are Micky Kearns on tenor saxophone – a former member of The Shufflers Sound Gaz and the Groovers and an extraordinary band called Supercharge; Jimmy on drums – also with Bernie and The Buzz Band; Gaffer on tenor saxophone – also a member of The Shufflers Sound; Keith on bass guitar – a former member of The Harlems; Willie Osu on lead guitar – also a member of The Buzz Band and an excellent guitarist (I played with him on a couple of occasions myself); and finally, Ray on guitar. On the front line, from left to right, are The Buzz Brothers, Bobby Wenton, Willie Wenton and Bernie Wenton. The Shufflers also backed The Buzz Brothers and Bernie was also the front man for Bernie's Buzz Band. The group decided to turn pro and signed up with Don Arden's management. They hit the London scene alongside groups like Jimmy James and the Vagabonds, The Nice and Skip Bifferty. They also got into the recording side of the business, releasing a song called *Don't Knock It*, on the D Ram label (DM 181.1968). They also released *The House that Jack Built*, on the Decca label (F.22829.1968).

Just Us was another group that Bernie played with. Their line-up was Jan Shelish, Jimmy Turner, Geoff Edmondson, Andy and Dave O'Hagan and Geoff Howarth. However, the group that I think made the biggest impact was The Shufflers Sound, along with the Buzz Brothers. The Buzz Brothers always had excellent musicians behind them and The Shufflers were no exception. On drums they had Alan (Zeff) on drums, Tony Gobie on bass, S Chantre on guitar, Ivor Ally on keyboards and Mick Kearns on tenor saxophone, eventually to be replaced by Gaffer.

Bernie won the television talent show, *Stars in Their Eyes,* as Nat King Cole. Until his death, Bernie was still a devoted fan of Nat King Cole and did a lot of charity work impersonating him. On the same bill, in the last charity event in which I saw Bernie appear, were The Merseybeats, The Real Thing and one of Liverpool's greatest Rock and Roll groups, Karl Terry and the Cruisers. It was Bernie who told me about a well-known character called Ralph (Pee-Wee) Spencer, or 'The Liverpool 8 Barber', who had just passed away. A community musician and entertainer, Pee-Wee's barbershop was a meeting place for boxers and musicians alike and he always had a couple of guitars hanging on the wall. On one occasion, a guitarist by the name of Charlie Jenkins called into the shop for a haircut on his way to work. Halfway through the cut, Pee-Wee decided to get the guitar down off the wall, and strum his way through his repertoire. Charlie ended up having to go to work with half a haircut, or he would have been late. Ralph Spencer is a character who will be missed by the community.

The Big Three

The Big Three were already a well-established trio around Liverpool, when Paddy Chambers on guitar and Faron on bass guitar joined them at the end of 1963 from Faron's Flamingos. The Big Three originally started out as Cass and the Casanovas, with Brian Casser on rhythm guitar / vocals, Johnny Hutchinson on drums / vocals, Johnny Gustafson on bass guitar and Adrian Barber on lead guitar. Adrian was quite at home with the electronics side of PA systems and amplifiers, and became quite well known around the Liverpool music scene for his famous coffin-style speaker cabinets, which gave the band their unique sound. Brian Casser soon decided to leave Liverpool and eventually ended up down in London under the name of Casey Jones, gigging with some first rate musicians such as Eric Clapton.

The rest of the group re-established themselves, forming The Big Three. With some outstanding Rock and Roll guitar riffs, they became a leading light amongst the Merseybeat groups and were eventually booked at the Star Club in Hamburg. They were a real powerhouse group and the German audiences loved them. Adrian Barber enjoyed the German lifestyle, so when offered the stage management job at the Star Club, he jumped at the chance, leaving Brian Griffiths in sole charge of the guitar work. Brian had left a well known group from Liverpool called Howie Casey and the Seniors (previously Derry Wilkie and the Seniors), the first of many Liverpool groups to play in Hamburg. Their line-up was made up of musicians such as Howie Casey – a tremendous saxophone player; Derry on lead vocals; Frank Wibberly on drums; Phil Whitehead on bass; Freddie Fowell on vocals; and Brian on lead guitar. The Seniors also released three singles and an LP, *Twist at the Top*, for the Fontana label. As you can see, Brian had quite a good pedigree behind him, but it was all to no avail when Howie Casey and the Seniors decided to split up. This would be around mid-summer 1962. Freddie Fowell later changed his name and became Freddie Starr and the Midnighters.

The Big Three went under the management of Brian Epstein, who secured television coverage and recording deals. They were on a high, with plenty of tour work. Despite this, Johnny Gustafson and Brian Griffiths pulled out of the group and teamed up with drummer Ian Broad to form a new group called The Seniors and went to play in Germany. This left an opening for Paddy Chambers and Faron. The group carried on under the name The Big Three, with plenty of work and re-recording *Some Other Guy*. Paddy only stayed with the group for a few months before Paul Pilnick stepped in on guitar, playing with Johnny Hutchinson and Faron until the group disbanded. Johnny Hutchinson reformed the group with Roy Marshall and Barry Womersley in 1965, but to no avail. They were such a loud and exciting group that I often wondered if there was any significance in Paul Pilnick naming his new group Deaf School! Paul also had a spell with the All Stars and The Fix. The Big Three were definitely one the top ten groups to come out of Liverpool.

The Connoisseurs

Dave Kent's memories of the Connoisseurs revert back to before he joined the group. Dave had played guitar for a dance band at Burtons Chambers in Spellow Lane, Liverpool 4. He started playing Shadows material, and the audience was so impressed by this new sound that Dave put a group together, along with Johnny Templer on vocals, called The Classics. They played the rock nights for a couple of years.

Dave moved about a lot, playing with several groups like the Mersey Gamblers and The G-Men, gaining experience playing lead guitar until he settled in with The Connoisseurs, who had been together since 1962. The line-up was: Mike Harkess, Kenny London – who was influenced by Jazz, Joe Bower from the Four Jays and Bazz Davies. Dave joined as lead guitarist.

The Connoisseurs entered the Oxfam Beat and Blues Competition, where they beat over sixty groups in the Liverpool finals, which were held at the Cavern Club. The group went to London for the British finals, competing against ten other groups; quite an achievement, even though they were runners-up. The Connoisseurs came back satisfied with their performance but convinced they had more to offer. Dave believes today that if Vince Earl had been with them at that time, it may have been a different outcome at the London finals. Incidentally, on the judging panel were Ringo Starr, Cilla Black and Brian Epstein.

After Vince Earl was brought into the group, they took on a more confident style of playing with two prominent lead harmony singers out front. Vince's presence added polish and refinement to the act. He was a competent performer, having just left Rory Storm and the Hurricanes, with whom he had played bass and vocals. Prior to joining The Hurricanes, Vince had been with The Talismen and also a group called The Zeros. The Connoisseurs finally answered the call to Germany and ended up in Hamburg for a three month stay. Whilst there, they met up with another Liverpool group, Ian and the Zodiacs, at the Pacific Hotel in Hamburg. The Connoisseurs never released any records, although they made many demo recordings for both PYE and George Martin.

When the Connoisseurs split up, Dave went with a group called The Brooklands and Vince joined The Attraction. The Connoisseurs will be remembered as another good group that should have made it. With the right record deal, they undoubtedly could have.

Sonny Webb and the Cascades

Kenny Johnson started out in 1959 in a group playing the same kind of material as most of the other groups. Then they became interested in the fringes of Country and Western and gradually became more involved in it. They played as The Country Four, but vocalist Kenny Johnson fell out with the group and left, later settling with The Wildcats, who had John State on guitar, Roger Wilcox on drums, Billy Duncan on bass guitar and Jerry Gilbertson on guitar. Kenny slotted in on guitar and vocals and Sonny Webb and the Cascades became the group's new name. They decided to go down the Rock and Roll road, but still tried to maintain a Country feel.

The group were just starting to get some recognition on the Liverpool scene, when Jerry Gilbertson left The Cascades, later followed by Billy Duncan. It was then that Joe Butler joined, previously having played with Kenny, and took on the role of bass guitarist. The group were certainly good enough to hold their own on the Merseybeat scene and received plenty of coverage in the local papers, *The Merseybeat* and The *Liverpool Echo*. Out of this varied collaboration of Country, Rock and Roll and Merseybeat, came one of Britain's most outstanding Country groups, The Hillsiders, who won over Country audiences in both England and Europe and also made a name for themselves in America. The line-up, when Kenny Johnson finally left the group, was Frank Wan on pedal steel guitar, Brian Redman on drums (Brian had played with the Four Jays and Kingsize Taylor and the Dominoes), and on guitar was Brian Hilton from the offspring group of The Remo Four – Group One. Kenny later formed a group called Kenny Johnson and the Northwind, who also made quite a name for themselves on the Country circuit.

As Sonny Webb and the Cascades, they had a single out on the Oriole label, *You've Got Everything / Boarder of the Blues*. The group also featured on *This is Merseybeat,* which was recorded live at the Rialto Ballroom in Liverpool. The song also featured on an EP called *Take Six*, which was a spin-off from This is Merseybeat. Today, both Kenny and Joe host their own country spot on local Liverpool radio. I apologise to those people whose names I have missed. Sadly, Joe Butler has passed away since this was written.

The Clayton Squares

Arthur Meskell and Billy Strand formed the Clayton Squares in late 1959. Completing their line-up were Eddie Caness and Bobby Scott. The group started rehearsing in a basement in Huskisson Street and were managed by George Roberts, who also introduced an alto-saxophone player, Mike Evans, into the group. Les Smith then joined on tenor saxophone and Terry Hynes on rhythm guitar / vocals. Arthur Meskell was on bass guitar and Bobby Scott on drums. The group rehearsed with this line-up for about nine months. Their first booking was for Allan Williams at the Blue Angel Club. A guitarist by the name of Eddie Williams joined the group for a short spell, but was replaced by Pete Dunn, who played keyboards and guitar and had previously played with a group called The Flintstones. Typical of other Merseybeat bands, the line-up was extremely fluid and members came and went. Accordingly, Terry Hynes suddenly left the group one day and never returned, later emerging with a group called The Fix and Denny Alexander came from the Kinsleys to replace him on guitar / vocals.

The group signed up with Cavern Artists, run by Ray McFall and Bob Wooler, playing at the Cavern Club quite regularly, where they built up a huge following. The year 1964 first took the group to Germany, the first of many visits, but they still came back to play the Cavern, where they also rehearsed. Saxophone player, Johnny Phillips, joined them for a short time, also playing with the Roadrunners, another Liverpool Rhythm and Blues group. The group eventually went under the management of Don Arden, who ran Galaxy Entertainment in Carnaby Street, in London, as well as groups like The Small Faces and The Nashville Teens. Nevertheless, the breaks still never came. However, the group did have a couple of records out for Decca: *Come and Get It* and the follow up, *There She Is*.

The Clayton Squares finally disbanded in September 1966. Their final line-up was Albie Donnelly on tenor saxophone, Geoff Jones on bass guitar, Bobby Scott on drums, Denny Alexander on vocals, Tony Priestly (former Realms guitarist) on guitar and Mike Evans on alto saxophone. Mike Evans later teamed up with Adrian Henri, the poet and singer with The Liverpool Scene. The group later reformed for a short spell as The Squares, with Karl Terry and guitarist Lance Railton, who joined them for a three-month stint in Spain, and six months in Germany.

The Clayton Squares were one of the most exciting Rhythm and Blues groups to watch in Liverpool, especially when they played at the Cavern. They were also the first group to record at the Cavern sound recording studio, which was based at the Cavern from October 1964. Bobby Scott, the original drummer with the group, reintroduced the original name as Bobby Scott's Clayton Squares, but with a different line-up: Tommy Nester on lead guitar, George Sloan on rhythm guitar, Bill Howard on bass guitar, Eric Woolley on lead / rhythm synthesizer guitar and Bobby Scott on drums. In recent years, the group have performed with American artist Bobby Vee, who came to fame when he became lead singer of The Crickets, after Buddy Holly lost his life in a plane crash. They also supported Chris Montez, who made the British charts with *Let's Dance*, in 1962, and Johnny Preston, who had a British number one with *Running Bear*, in February 1960. They also supported PJ Proby, who made it into the charts with *Hold Me*, on Decca, in 1964, reaching number three. On the same show were The Merseybeats, who first made the British charts in 1963 with *It's Love that Really Counts* on Fontana, as well as numerous other artists. They are also part of Merseycats children's charity.

KARL TERRY AND THE CRUISERS

Karl Terry and the Cruisers were renowned for their entertainment value. They played with all the Liverpool hit-making groups such as The Searchers and The Beatles, plus many others. Karl Terry was one of the great showmen of the sixties. He fronted The Cruisers who, in the photograph, consisted of Gerry Clayton, Don McCormack, Gordon Templeton, Laurie Clark and Dave Hamilton. Les Braid had previously played with Karl, eventually leaving the group to be replaced by Dave Hamilton. Les ended up later in The Swinging Blue Jeans as the bass player. Karl, over the years, has played alongside some of Merseyside's top musicians, such as Paddy Chambers, Lance Railton and Roy Dyke, to name but a few.

Although Karl never made it to super star level like The Beatles, or Gerry Marsden, he has always been a prominent figure on the Rock and Roll scene in and around Liverpool. In a recent conversation with him, he told me how Tony Crane and Billy Kinsley nearly joined the group. The Cruisers had been offered the chance of some bookings abroad playing for the American forces, but there was some controversy over permits, as some of the lads were deemed too young to go. Eventually, Tony and Billy decided against it, so Geoff Caddick and a girl called Nicolette Moran went instead. Whilst they were over there, Paddy Chambers joined them. Able to play both bass and guitar, Karl played with other prominent groups around Liverpool, spending some time with Rory Storm and the Hurricanes and Group One, to mention only two. Karl is one of the true gentlemen of Rock and Roll and he and the Cruisers put a lot of time into doing charity shows for Merseycats.

Billy Kramer and the Coasters

Billy Kramer and the Coasters originally started out in 1960 as The Sand Stormers, later changing their name to The Phantoms. Billy, whose real name is William Howard Ashton, played guitar with the group accompanied by Ray Doughty on lead guitar; George Braithwaite on bass guitar and Tony Sanders on drums. The reason Billy became front man with the group was purely accidental; his guitar was stolen and his cousin, Arthur Ashton, who was a friend of Mike Pender of The Searchers, stepped in for him on rhythm guitar, leaving Billy out front as lead vocalist. The group went on playing until 1963, when Billy was on the verge of going professional. Problematically, The Coasters were not. George and Ray were still serving a trade and so they parted company. Billy continued with The Dakotas as his backing group, bringing out their first record *Do You Want to Know a Secret?* The Coasters later teamed up with Chick Graham. They blended well to become Chick Graham and the Coasters.

Chick Graham and the Coasters were taken under the wing of Decca, when the group decided they were ready to turn professional. Their line-up was Chick Graham on lead vocals, Arthur Ashton on lead guitar, Ray Dougherty on rhythm guitar, Tony Sanders on drums, George Braithwaite – who had been with The Coasters from early on – played bass guitar but decided not to turn professional and so left the group. Ray Dougherty later gave up the rhythm guitar and went on to bass. The group released their first single, *I Know / Education*, followed by *A little You / Dance Baby, Dance.*

Meanwhile, Billy J Kramer and the Dakotas were on a roll under the management of Brian Epstein and a recording deal with Parlophone. Their releases included, *Do You Want to Know a Secret? Bad to Me, I'll Keep You Satisfied, Little Children, From a Window, It's Gotta Last Forever* and *Trains and Boats and Planes*. Billy was nearing the end of his roll in the charts with *Neon City*. He released five EPs for Parlophone, and an LP with The Dakotas called *Listen*. Billy J Kramer now resides in America but visits Liverpool whenever he gets the chance.

JASON EDDIE AND THE CENTREMEN

Albie Wycherley, the younger brother of Billy Fury, was introduced to the Centremen through the group's drummer. At that time they had a female vocalist called Beryl, hence the name, Beryl and the Centremen. Albie knew the drummer through working at St John's Market and he told Albie that the group were looking for a new singer. Albie made arrangements to drop in at one of the lads' houses to run through some of their songs. They were impressed with him and started him off by just doing three songs at the first gig, then six at the next gig, and so on. The group then went out as The Centremen and not long afterwards, Albie changed his name to Al Trent. Interestingly, just before Albie joined The Centremen, he had been introduced to Joe Meek, through Freddie Starr, who had talked him into driving him down to London to see Joe, as Freddie had just recorded a song for him called *Who Told You*. Freddie introduced Albie to Joe, explaining that he was Billy Fury's brother and Joe asked him to record a couple of songs for him at his studio. He then advised him to go back to Liverpool and join a group to get some experience behind him, and then get back in touch.

This brings us up to date with Albie, who by this time was fronting Al Trent and the Centremen. The group played all the major venues, gaining as much experience as they could. Albie then got back in touch with Joe Meek, who recorded the group singing a cover version of the Tommy Steel song *Singing the Blues*, that reached number 44 in the charts for a couple of weeks, also a song called *What You Gonna Do, Baby*? The group had a few more tracks ready to be released, when, sadly, Joe decided to end his own life. As Joe had operated as an independent company, the contracts of the other group members were terminated immediately.

The group went on to tour the country with people like The Walker Brothers and The Troggs, but they decided to call it a day in 1968. It was around 1972 that Jason Eddie came back on the scene with one of the original members of The Centremen, who had been working with the resident group at the Castaways Club in Runcorn. The group got together with Albie and formed the Jason Eddie Sound. I saw them playing at the Star and Garter Club in Liverpool, in the early 1970s, and they were an impressive live band. Albie has been involved in many charity shows over the years and also recordings for numerous charity organisations. *The Class of 64* albums are a good example of his work. He still gets involved with the Billy Fury fan club and can also be found on the Joe Meek Rarities album. He still sounds good today.

KINGSIZE TAYLOR AND THE DOMINOES

We now go back to 1957, when The Dominoes were first formed. They came from the Litherland, Crosby and Seaforth areas of Liverpool. The group members consisted of Arthur Baker, who was the vocalist in the group; on piano, from Crosby, was Sam Hardie and on the guitar was Charlie Flynn along with George Watson, and Cliff Roberts on drums. Incidentally, the group was Cliff's brainchild.

Their focus was Rock and Roll and they started to get gigs around the Crosby and Seaforth area. At one of their gigs they were on with another group called The James Boys, who were a Skiffle based group. In their line-up was guitarist Teddy Taylor, who was impressed with The Dominoes and their style of music. By 1958, Teddy Taylor was playing guitar and vocals for the Dominoes. Shortly after, Charlie was called up to do his National Service and had to leave the group, only able to do the odd gig when he was home on leave. George also left the group and joined The Vince Diamond Trio, but the vacancy was soon to be filled by Bobby Thompson on bass, who was formerly a member of The James Boys. The line-up was now taking on a new dimension, as the vocals were getting tighter. The next change came in 1959, when Sam Hardie decided to leave the group to join the Police Force. The next new addition was Johnny Kennedy on guitar / vocals, who will be remembered for his spell with The Zodiacs and who added further vocals to the line-up.

The group was to have another change, this time not in the line-up, but in the name of the group. Teddy Taylor was to front the group as Kingsize Taylor, the name Kingsize supposedly a reference to a new type of cigarette that had just come on the market, but Teddy told me that the promoter, Brian Kelly, of Bee-Kay Promotions, had actually taken the name from a children's television cartoon show. In any event, the group were to go under the name Kingsize Taylor and the Dominoes, a name still talked about today in musical circles with admiration. Charlie Flynn was reintroduced and the group took off with a vengeance, playing all the major venues around Liverpool.

By 1962, the magnetism of Hamburg was too strong and the group were eventually drawn to Germany but without the presence of Cliff Bennet and Johnny Kennedy; Charlie, Flynn, Dave Lovelady and John Frankland, going in their places. Dave stayed for a couple of months when a swap with The Four Jays' drummer Brian Redman was made.

The group stayed on in Germany alongside many great American stars, making a name for themselves as one of the best groups to come out of Merseyside. They were to have another change in the line-up when Brian Redman left and Gibson Kemp stepped in to play the drums. They also got themselves a saxophone player, Howie Casey, who came from The Seniors. The Dominoes made many recordings as Kingsize Taylor and the Dominoes and they also recorded for Polydor under the name The Shakers. They had a number one hit in Germany with *Stupidity*. All in all, they remain one of the finest Rock and Roll groups of that era and a credit to Liverpool.

The Dennisons

The Dennisons, as Ray Scragg the guitarist / vocalist with the group so rightly said, "Were a group's group", which I think sums them up. Sadly, not all the members are with us today, but they are still remembered in the history of the sixties, as we travel back in time to those golden years. Many people were puzzled by the origin of the name, The Dennisons. It came to light during a conversation with Ray that the name had apparently come from a style of shoe found in a certain Liverpool shoe shop. The group's drummer, Clive Hornby, went on to further his career in the world of television, better known to his soap fans as Jack Sugden, from Emmerdale.

The Dennisons were a popular group, even when they played on the same bill as Gerry and the Pacemakers and The Beatles, who they used to support on a Sunday night at the Opera House in Blackpool. The Dennisons had chart hits themselves with songs such as *Be My Girl*, which got into the top 40, *Ain't Nobody Like My Baby* and *Walking the Dog*, which got into the top 30, and featured Ray on lead vocals. The Rolling Stones also had success in the charts with that song. Incidentally the group had a song written for them by Ben E King.

Like many groups around at the time, their recordings were all live.

The Dennisons recorded *Always Devoted to You* and *You'd Better Move On*, live at the Cavern, but unfortunately Decca seem to have lost the original tapes. Ray Scragg has also sadly passed away. In my own opinion, they should have made a bigger impact on the music scene than they did.

The Easybeats

The Easybeats' original line-up, in 1963, was Frank Townsend playing guitar, Jimmy Doran, Frank McTigue and Frank Cork. The group made quite a name for themselves around Liverpool, playing alongside many top Liverpool artists. After a time, Frank Cork decided to quit the band, leaving an opening for a drummer, which was filled by Pete Ore. This line-up stayed the same till around 1965. The group changed its name to The Dealers for a short while but soon reverted to The Easybeats. Kit Lambert was their manager (and also The Who). Then Frank Townsend left the group and stepped in with The Escorts and Terry Sylvester had already left to join The Swinging Blue Jeans and later The Hollies.

The line-up of The Escorts was Frank Townsend guitar / organ / vocals, John Kinrade on lead guitar, Tommy Kelly on drums and Mike Gregory on bass guitar / vocals. Like so many others, the group signed up to play in Germany. On his return, it was Frank's intention to rejoin The Easybeats again with Jimmy Doran, but he received a phonecall from Al Isenberg, asking him to join Tony Rivers and the Castaways instead, with whom he stayed for approximately a year. Frank then returned to Liverpool and formed a group called The Beechwoods, who styled themselves on The Beach Boys, as Frank was an ardent Beach Boys fan. The line-up of this band was Frank Townsend on guitar / vocals, John Larkin on lead vocals, Jimmy Doran on guitar, Eddy Edwards on drums and George Cassidy on bass guitar. The group recorded an LP, *Hits of The Beach Boys*, as *Taste of Honey*. The group were together from around 1967 till 1971. Frank later joined up with a group called Ocean for a while, and also played with Billy Kinsley from The Merseybeats, who formed a group called Liverpool Express. Frank did manage to reform his old group The Easybeats for a few gigs in the late1990s. Listen out for Frank's excellent vocals on *The Class of 64* CDs.

BILLY FURY

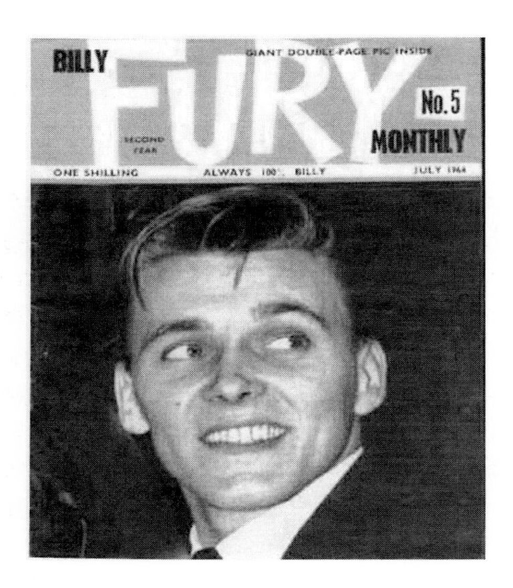

Born on 17 April 1940, in Liverpool, Ronald Wycherley was brought up in the Dingle area of the city. Ronnie had rheumatic fever at the age of six, which left him with a serious heart disorder. On leaving school, Ronnie acquired a job working as a deckhand on a tugboat on the River Mersey. Although it was an arduous job, he was strong willed and struggled on, despite his weak heart. Music was a big influence in his life and he made his first attempts at recording in 1958, with an acetate record, accompanying himself on the guitar at Philips recording studio in

Kensington, Liverpool. He also made his debut at the Empire Theatre, in Lime Street, when he auditioned for the Carrol Levis Talent Show. Ronnie eventually managed to audition for Larry Parnes at the Essoldo Theatre, in Birkenhead. On the bill at the time was Marty Wilde. Ronnie made a lasting impression on both Marty and Larry Parnes, who brought him into his stable of stars and christened him with the dynamic new stage name, Billy Fury. His song-writing skills had not gone unnoticed either and his first single, *Maybe Tomorrow,* which he wrote himself, was released for Decca. It went into the charts in February 1959, reaching number 22. That single re-entered the charts on 27 March 1959, reaching number six. There was also a follow-up single in 1959 with *Margo,* which peaked at number 28 in the charts.

Billy became a star almost overnight and worked alongside such stars as Eddie Cochran and Gene Vincent. On 10 May 1960, Larry Parnes held auditions because Billy needed a backing group for touring, The Beatles turned up at the audition, but on this occasion they were taken on as a backing group for another of Larry Parnes' stars, Johnny Gentle, who toured Scotland. 1960 also saw the release of a memorable LP, *The Sound of Fury*, that was released on 4 June 1960 and stayed at number 18 in the charts for two weeks.

One of the highlights of Billy's career was in 1962, when he presented Elvis Presley with two silver UK discs (Billy was a huge fan of Elvis). Also, that same year, Billy was featured in his first film *Play It Cool,* along with Bobby Vee and Helen Shapiro, featuring hits like *Once Upon a Dream, Play It Cool, You're Swell, Who Can Say? Cry My Heart Out, At a Time Like This* and *But I Don't Care*. From 1962 to 1965, Billy was still releasing memorable singles but still failed to reach the number one slot in the charts, with songs like *I Will* and *Like I've Never Been Gone*.

Billy had a second film release – *I've Got a Horse*. The film was based around his own involvement with racehorses, in fact his own horse, Anselmo, was in the frame in the 1964 Derby. It was Billy's love of horses and animals that encouraged him to start his own wild-life farm, working closely with the RSPCA. Meanwhile, Billy's heart problem had not gone away and led to a series of operations. He was pushed more and more into the cabaret and pantomime side of the business and unfortunately his change of record label did nothing to help his career, but he was to be featured in another film, *That'll Be the Day*.

In January of 1983 things started looking brighter for Billy; there was a forthcoming tour with Helen Shapiro and he was also working on material in the recording studio. However, Billy suddenly became seriously ill and later sadly passed away – the end of a star and a music legend. The Billy Fury Fan Club have raised money for a statue in honour of Billy in Liverpool, supported by Billy's mother and also his younger brother, Albie Wycherley.

FARON'S FLAMINGOS

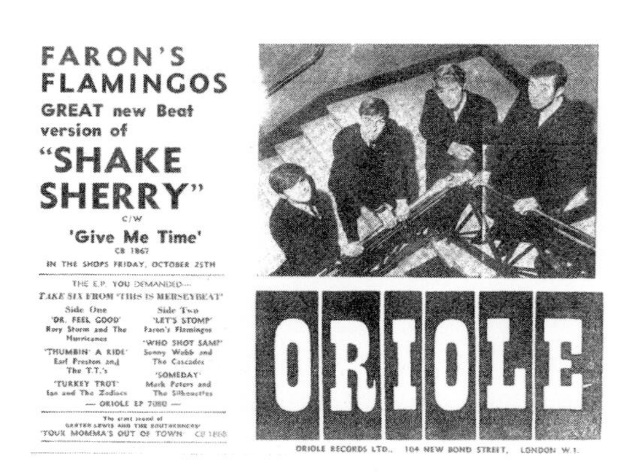

In 1959 a band started out as Johnny Tempest and the Tornadoes, with Johnny Tempest on vocals, Rod Cameron on drums, Lance Railton on lead guitar, Wally Shepard on bass guitar, Dave Gore on rhythm guitar and Faron on guitar / vocals. Sadly, Johnny Tempest died and so Faron moved out front, giving up the guitar to become lead vocalist. Then Rod left the band, leaving an opening for Don Alcyd. Faron then moved on from the Tempest Tornadoes to join up with Gerry Marsden and the Pacemakers to work in Germany. Earl Preston and Cy Tucker replaced Faron, under the name Earl Preston and the TTs. Things did not work out with The Pacemakers in Germany, due to a conflict of personalities within the group.

When Faron returned to Liverpool, he went to work for Wally Hill as a compere at Blair Hall, a dance hall in Walton Road, Liverpool, and it was there that he came into contact with The Ravens. Their lead singer, Robin, had failed to turn up, so the group asked Faron if he would stand in on vocals. He did so and was asked to stay on with them under the name of Faron and the Ravens.

The group were playing at the Aintree institute when Bob Wooler came down to the club looking for a job, because he had fallen out with promoter Wally Hill. He asked Faron to introduce him to Brian Kelly, which

Faron did. One day Nicky Crouch and Bob Wooler were standing at a bus stop discussing a new name for the group, when Bob came up with Faron's Flamingos, so Bob took the credit for the group's name. Faron's Flamingos recorded many songs including: *Shake Sherry, Let's Stomp, Do You Love Me? See if She Cares, Give Me Time, Talking About You* and *So Fine*. They turned down Decca to sign for Oriel, with tracks on *This is Merseybeat*. The group also played for the American forces in France.

Later on in his career, Faron went to live in France and made quite a name for himself over there. Faron's next move was with The Big Three. The final line-up of the Flamingos; was Faron, Paddy Chambers, Nicky Crouch and Trevor Morais. Prior to that line-up, Faron also had some excellent musicians in the group such as Eric London, Mushy Cooper and Billy Jones.

THE FOURMOST

Formerly The Four Jays, this group formed in 1959. Brian O'Hara was on lead guitar / vocals, Brian Redman on drums, Joe Bower on guitar / vocals and Billy Hatton on bass. They were making a good name for themselves until around 1962, when there was a problem over the name of the group, because there was another group around at that time with the same name. Along with a name change, eventually into The Fourmost, there was also a change in the line-up. Brian Redman was to leave for Germany for a three month swap with Dave Lovelady, to play with Kingsize Taylor and the Dominoes, on the understanding that, on his return, he would rejoin the group. However, when Brian returned he found there was no job for him, because Dave had fitted in so well. Bob Wooler was once again responsible for the introduction of a new name for the group – The Fourmost.

The group was eventually taken under the wing of Brian Epstein and produced some memorable recordings like *Hello Little Girl* and *A Little Loving*. The group had another change in the line-up when Mike Millward left, due to ill health. The newcomer was George Peckem, who had previously played with The Olympics, but his involvement was short term. This left an opening for Ian Edwards from The Zodiacs. Ian had spent quite some time over in Germany, but had returned to England after his wife had fallen ill. He soon settled in with The Fourmost and also with some recording work. On one track the keyboard player was Paul McCartney. Ian Edwards eventually decided to leave, making room for Joe Bower to come in again on guitar / vocals, just as he had in 1959, when the group first started out. The Fourmost stand out as one of Liverpool's best a cappella-style close harmony groups.

THE HIDEAWAYS

The Hideaways were a group with a unique sound and who featured in many star line-ups at the Cavern, along with Georgie Fame and the Blueflames, Sonny Boy Williamson, Ben E King, John Mayall's Blues Breakers, Spencer Davies and John Lee Hooker, the American Blues King ... the list goes on. The group was formed in December 1963, when they decided they were ready for some live gigs and went down to a club in Red

Cross Street, on the chance of a booking. When they were asked the name of the group, they realised they didn't have one, so glancing up at the club's name over the doorway – The Hideaway Club – they spontaneously said, "We're The Hideaways!" They must have gone down well, because they played as resident group throughout January and February.

The group, now into 1964, advertised for a saxophone player, but were answered by Judd Lander who only played the mouth organ. However, after hearing him play, he became the latest addition to The Hideaways. In fact, the Blues-influenced Judd became the mainstay of the group. They were introduced to Bob Wooler at the Cavern by Vic Wright, the lead singer with Vic and the Spidermen, who worked as a clothes buyer for the Ethel Austin warehouse in Derby Lane, Old Swan. Frankie Connor and John Donaldson also worked there as Vic's juniors. Their first booking at the Cavern was in March 1964 and the group received some recognition through a television advertisement for Timex watches, filmed at the club.

The Hideaways soon acquired a large following at the Cavern, and more or less became the resident group there from 1964 to 1970. Their line-up was Frankie Connor on rhythm guitar / vocals, John Donaldson on drums, Ozzie Yue on lead guitar / vocals, Judd Lander on harmonica / vocals and John Shell on bass guitar / vocals. Over the years, there were various changes to the line-up – John Donaldson left the group and was replaced by Phil Chittick and John Shell was drafted into the American forces, as he was classed as an American citizen. John was killed in action in 1968, which was a great loss to the local music scene. Chris Findley, who had previously played with The Merseys and The Mindbenders, replaced him. He was originally a keyboard player but went over to bass guitar when he joined The Hideaways.

The group were actually on the bill at the Cavern when it closed down in February 1966, making them the last group on stage, along with disc jockey, Billy Butler, when the authorities eventually gained access to the club the following morning. The Hideaways were also the first group back on stage when the club reopened its doors for business on 23 July 1966.

Around 1968 Judd Lander left and joined a group called Cellophane, and spent most of his time down in London. The group had material written for them by Albert Hammond and Tony Waddington and their first single was *Girl Called Fantasy*. Leapy Lee was another writer who got involved in writing for the group, contributing to the B-side with *Happiness Is Love*, which was released for the CBS label. Judd also got involved with session work for Apple, and was asked to play on John Lennon's Rock and Roll album. He now lives in London, where he works as a freelance session musician. Ozzie Yue also left the group for a while to join Edwin Starr's backing group, Cool Combination. He actually got the job through Phil Chan, who played with Rod Stewart. Ozzie rejoined The Hideaways and they released a single in 1970, recorded at the Sink Club in Liverpool, under the name of Confucius, for the RCA label. The A side was *The Brandenburg Concerto* and the B side *The Message*, written by Chris Finley and Frankie Connor. The group appeared at the Cavern Club over 300 times and stand out as one of the best Rhythm and Blues groups in Liverpool.

Rory Storm and The Hurricanes

The Hurricanes may have become one of Liverpool's outstanding Rock and Roll groups but they didn't start out that way. Forming in 1957 as a Skiffle group, they initially called themselves The Raving Texans. Alan Caldwell was the lead singer, and armed with tea-chest bass and washboard, the group set out to get bookings wherever they could and also entered the many Skiffle contests that were around at the time. The group won a holiday at Butlins at one such contest, sponsored by *The People* magazine. It was at Butlins that they came across their new vocation in life – to be a Rock and Roll group. This change of direction came about after watching the resident group, Rory Blackwell and the Blackjacks. Whilst there, Rory Blackwell asked John Byrne, the guitarist with The Texans, and another lad who was there at the time, Clive Powell, who played keyboards, to join his group. John declined, but Clive joined up with Rory Blackwell and travelled to London with him. Clive later changed his name to Georgie Fame.

When The Texans arrived back in Liverpool they had a different musical outlook, determined to be a Rock and Roll group. The first thing they needed was to find themselves a drummer, then some amplifiers. John bought himself an Antoria guitar from Rushworths, at a cost of £28, reckoning it was one of the first electric guitars in Liverpool. Having picked up a Framus bass guitar and three Selmer 'True Voice' amplifiers, their next task was to find a suitable drummer. They chose Ringo Starr, despite the fact that he only had an incomplete set of drums, but with the aid of Alan Caldwell, they managed to cobble together a full set.

The group began playing the local clubs and halls under the name Al Storm and the Hurricanes, later changing their name to Rory Storm and the Hurricanes. They decided it was time to approach George Gantry, Cliff Richard's agent, for an audition for Butlins. They eventually secured the audition, which was held at the Grafton Ballroom and which they passed. Cliff Richard and the Drifters went to Butlins in Clacton and The Hurricanes went to Butlins, Pwhelli. By this time, Butlins had a purpose-built ballroom, which was perfect, except for the gang fights, which inevitably broke out there. The group played another year at Pwhelli and then a third year at Butlins, Skegness, and it was at Skegness that Ringo was offered the chance to join The Beatles. Apparently, Rory's group recognised that The Beatles were going to make it to the big time and chose not to stand in his way.

In 1963, Rory Storm and The Hurricanes were recorded by Oriole. John Shroeder had brought a mobile recording studio to the Rialto Ballroom in Liverpool to record two live LPs of Liverpool groups entitled *This is Merseybeat*. Rory Storm and the Hurricanes were voted number four in the first Merseybeat polls, in 1961; third were The Remo Four, second were Gerry and the Pacemakers and the number one spot went to The Beatles. In 1964, Brian Epstein brought the group down to London, to EMI in Abbey Road, to record a couple of tracks: *America* and *Since You Broke My Heart*, released on Parlophone (R5197).

The group then saw the sad loss of two of its mainstay members, when Ty Brian died, followed by the death of Rory Storm himself, in September 1972. Rory Storm and the Hurricanes were one of the most exciting Merseybeat groups ever to perform on stage. Sadly Johnny Byrne (guitarist), who kindly gave me an interview, passed away in 1999.

The Harlems

Sugar Deen was always interested in music; his forte being vocal harmony singing. His early groups were The Earls and The Conquests, who rehearsed intensely in places like Stanley House. He also had a short spell with The Washington Soul Band, who were based in Gateacre, Liverpool. He then joined a group called The Valentinos, who also made vocal harmony the mainstay of their act. The group was a four-piece, with Eddie Williams, Laurence Areaty, Chris Smith and Tony Fayle. Chris left the group, making way for Sugar. Later, Vinny Ismayle from The Detours came in. The group played together for about eight years but they encountered a great deal of racism in Newcastle and the surrounding areas and the Valentinos eventually split up.

Sugar later formed a group called The Harlems; a similar style of group, with the emphasis on vocal harmony. The line-up was once again four-part harmony with Laurence Areaty, Barry Philbin, Vinny Ismayle and Sugar. Vinny then left and Mick Chong was brought in. They looked as good as they sounded – a well-rehearsed polished act. I saw the group just before they got through to the auditions for Hughie Green's *Opportunity Knocks*. The group had auditioned for the show three times and passed each time, only to be told that they could not be used on that occasion, but fourth time lucky, they got through to the show. Willy Osu introduced them to Hughie Green. I got to know Willy quite well over the years and played guitar with him on a couple of occasions. Just before the group went out on the set to do their spot, a lady who was involved in the organisation backstage said to the lads, "Just go out there and do your best. Don't be disappointed if you don't win; it's who sees you out there that matters." The Harlems went out and performed their act live.

Although they didn't win, the group started getting plenty of work under the wing of agent, Mickey Heyes and went into recording, cutting some demos for Polydor and also releasing a single for Dick James called *It Takes a Fool Like Me*. In my opinion, The Harlems should have made it in the recording scene, and achieved the success of their old friends The Chants. In the late 1970s, Tony Fayle sadly passed away, which was a great loss, as he was a member of both The Valentinos and The Harlems; also Willy Osu, and more recently Vinny Ismayle, they will all be missed from the local music scene.

The Hy-Tones

Stan Johnson, guitarist with the group, remembers starting rehearsing sometime in 1957, at his father's laundrette in Dinas Lane, Huyton, hence the name The Hy-tones. The group practised for about three months before they felt ready to face the local music scene. The original members were Billy Hughes on bass / vocals, Jimmy O'Connor on vocals / guitar, Derrick Gill on drums, Stan Foster on piano and Stan Johnson on rhythm guitar. The group auditioned for the local agents, establishing themselves as a Rock and Roll group around Liverpool. After a while, the group brought in saxophone player, Howie Casey, who had just left the army and not long after that, a young singer called Derry Wilkie joined the group as lead vocalist. The next addition was a lead guitarist, Brian Griffiths, who was an outstanding musician, Stan was not sure who introduced him to the group. It could have been either Derry or Howie. Brian only stayed with the group for a short while, as he was involved in an accident at the Lybro factory where he worked, injuring his fingers.

Stan gave us a list of the clubs in which The Hy-Tones played during his time with the group: The English Electric Club, Blair Hall, The Pavilion, Lodge Lane, Litherland Town Hall, Moss Bank Labour Club, St Helens, St Luke's, Crosby, Knotty Ash Village Hall, Orrell Park Ballroom, The Cavern Club, Hollyoake Hall, Smithdown Road, The Rialto Ballroom, Princes Road, The Automatic Telephone Club, Huyton, The Tent, Huyton Quarry and Sutton Manor Miners' Club, St Helens. Sutton Manor coal mine was also Stan Johnson's place of work as a young man.

When the group eventually split up in the early 1960s, Howie took what was left of the group and formed The Seniors.

THE IN CROWD

Arrangements were made to interview Karl Terry in a nightclub in Liverpool, where he was playing for a charity show on the same bill as The Merseybeats and The Real Thing. I also met George Dixon, better known for his years with, from a musician's point of view, one of the best harmony groups to come out of Liverpool. George gave me the story of how he became a member of The In Crowd, going back to when he came out of the army in 1958, and remembers the good times he had singing in the Grafton Ballroom. We go back to the Skiffle and Jazz band days when George decided to get back into music and started playing guitar with friends Wally Quarles and Norman Frazer. Perfectionists, they would practise a song for weeks on end until it was exactly right, and eventually got their first booking at the White House in Liverpool, where their first payment was about four pounds. They were well received and asked to play Friday to Monday every week.

After a while, word spread amongst the local groups and many of them would come and watch them on Monday nights. In particular, two lads used to come and watch them play, always dressed in black, from a new group called The Beatles.

George and the rest of the lads stayed at the White House for about four or five years, then Norman Frazer decided that it was time to leave. At about the same time, George was taking saxophone lessons and it was during these that he met up with Gerry Stewart, who had been playing with Blues groups around Liverpool in places like The Blue Angel Club. Gerry eventually joined up with George and they then brought in Gerry's brother-in-law, who was a member of The Black Cats. They appeared under many names such as The Casuals and The Takeria All-stars. During this time George had heard of a group called The Beatles who were looking for a singer, but he decided against approaching them and carried on playing with Gerry and Dave instead. The group played together for a couple of years until Dave and Gerry both decided to leave.

A new group was then formed when Tony Fayle joined the group as lead singer and with the introduction of John Carney, George and Wally, they formed The In Crowd. The group then took on the residency at the Masonic in Liverpool for a couple of years. John Carney then left and was replaced by Tony Adams. Tony at that time was only sixteen years old, but had an outstanding voice. The group turned professional and went on tour in Europe. George then decided that he needed a break and had a rest from playing for about eighteen months. In 1971 he joined a group called Just Us with Willie Wenton, Ken Ross, Dave Stead and Eric Hanson. The group played together until 1976.

Dale Roberts and the Jaywalkers

The Jaywalkers were another local group active on the Liverpool scene. Formed in 1959, they gained experience through playing local halls and clubs and trying their luck on talent contests such as the Carrol Levis Shows, that were held at The Empire in Liverpool. They also backed people such as Lance Fortune, who made it into the charts with a song called *Be Mine*. The group deservedly gained popularity with the audience, as well as the respect of other groups. Dale Roberts was lead singer and the band was to be one of the earlier groups to play at the Cavern.

When Rock and Roll began to take off, audiences wanted more of such groups as Dale Roberts and the Jaywalkers and Rory Storm and the Hurricanes, to play the Cavern. The other group members were Dave Williams on lead guitar, Bill Buck on drums, Phil Rogers on bass guitar / vocals and Ian Boyle on rhythm guitar. They played the Cavern Club on Tuesday, 21 March 1961, on the Blue Genes guest night, along with The Remo Quartet and The Beatles, making their first evening appearance. Phil eventually left the group and joined The Remo Four (originally The Remo Quartet). Dave also left and formed a new group, along with Harry Prytherch and Keith Stokes, who were formerly with The Remo Four. They also brought in Eric London from Faron's Flamingos on bass guitar, calling themselves Group One. In 1964, Dave then left the group and joined Dale Roberts, in a group called The Four Originals, who are still playing sixties music around Liverpool and Wirral. Dave Williams, Harry Prytherch and Eric London are all members of Merseycats.

THE KRUZADS

Ken (Dixie) Dean was originally a member of Gerry Marsden's Skiffle group in the late 1950s. They played the Pavillion in Liverpool for a week in a show called Dublin to Dingle. The group also won a Skiffle contest at the Woolton Labour Club against stiff competition, because also taking part were The Quarry Men. In the 1960s, Dixie and Eddie Hill formed a group called the Kruzads, who made their debut in the Cavern Club on Wednesday, 17 June 1964. The group played the Cavern about eight times, altogether. They received some good reviews supporting groups like Manfred Mann and The Pretty Things, at the Tower Ballroom, New Brighton, compered by Billy Butler.

The group toured with The Merseybeats, The Escorts and The Kinsleys and also with The Croupiers and The Valkyries, along with Kenny Lynch and the Echos on The Mersey Sound Package. In the line-up, along with Dixie, was Eddie Hill on bass guitar, Billy Roberts on lead guitar (who had also played with a group called The City Beats, and who came third in the Frankie Vaughn Talent Competition, which was held at Crane Hall; first place went to Denny Seyton and the Sabres and second place went to The Senators). The youngest member of the group was Danny Bell on drums, aged just thirteen! They were classed as Liverpool's answer to The Rolling Stones, although they claim that they never tried to emulate The Stones, there was just a similarity in both their styles of music. When the group played a late night gig they had to have a change of drummer at certain venues after ten thirty, owing to Danny's age! Bass player Arthur Meskell was later brought into the group to replace Eddie, having previously played for The Clayton Squares. The group made quite a name for themselves in France and Belgium, where they lived for quite a while. The lead guitarist with the group, Billy Roberts, went on to be a psychic and medium and appears at theatres up and down the country. Billy recently reformed The Kruzads to perform in the show, with the line-up of Dixie Dean, Paul Hitchmough, Jimmy Ikonomides, Steve Doyle and Billy Roberts himself. Sadly, I was informed that Eddie Hill, the bass guitarist with the group, has recently died.

The Liverpool Scene

Mike Evans left the Clayton Squares and eventually ended up with The Liverpool Scene. However, before that, a group was formed for a three-month stint in Madrid, amalgamated from The Clayton Squares and The TTs. Their line-up was Lance Railton on guitar, Alby Donnelly on saxophone, Mike Evans also on saxophone, Geoff Jones on bass guitar, Tommy McGuire on drums and Karl Terry on vocals. When they arrived in Madrid they were billed as Con-y-Plaza's Karl Terry and the Squares. The roadie with the group was Billy Johnson, who bought an old Standard Atlas van for the trip. A similar line-up, in January 1967, spent six months in Frankfurt. The group returned to Liverpool on the same day as The Beatles released their *Sergeant Pepper* album.

In June 1967, Mike Evans teamed up with The Liverpool Poets, with well-known artist-come-poet Adrian Henri and Andy Roberts on guitar. In September 1967, they were billed at the Edinburgh Festival as The Liverpool Scene. Their name was taken from a book of poetry and the name stayed with the band. In October 1967, Mike took up a permanent position with The Liverpool Scene, along with Adrian Henri, Andy Roberts, Mike Hart (formerly in The Road Runners), Brian Dobson (formerly with Rogues Gallery and Earthlings) on drums, and Percy Jones on bass guitar. In September 1968, the group became involved with RCA and released an album, *The Incredible Adventures*. A second album was released in June / July 1969, called *Bread on the Night*. They were signed up from September to November 1969 as the support band to Led Zeppelin on the UK Isle of Wight tour. A third album was released in early 1970, entitled *St Adrian's Company Broadway and Third*. The Liverpool Scene decided to call it a day in March 1970. Sadly, both Lance Railton and Adrian Henri are no longer with us.

The Merseybeats

The first actual gig that Billy ever did was with John Banks and Nicky Bruntskill, on Boxing Day night, 1960, for the mother of one of their friends, Kenny Wheel, who owned a carpet shop in Kensington. It was not until mid-1961 that the Merseybeats got together, but before going under that name they were called The Mavericks, which stems back to the Ranking Boys' Club, where Billy was a member of the running team. He formed The Mavericks with Tony Crane on guitar, Frank Sloane on drums and Billy on bass guitar. The leader of the boys' club suggested they should hold a dance at the club, which was not only a first for the group, but also a first for the club, as girls were to be allowed in. The lads set about redecorating the club and even arranging separate toilets for the girls. A make-shift stage was formed out of metal crisp boxes, with a plinth laid across them. The show was set for Friday night – The Mavericks' first gig – but Tony Crane decided he was not ready to play and stood down, leaving Billy and Frank to fulfil the booking, supported by two lads out of Billy's cousin's group. Despite such last minute complications, the group played well. Tony was there on the night and saw how the audience appreciated them and decided to play the following week, which was really their first proper gig as The Mavericks.

The group eventually brought Dave Elias into the group, making them up to a four-piece. Bob Wooler started to take an interest and got them a few gigs around the coffee houses and suburban dance halls and it was Bob who actually gave the group the name The Merseybeats, which was taken from *The Merseybeat*, a local music magazine. They played the Aintree Institute three weeks on the run, the first week as The Mavericks, the second week as The Pacifics and the third week as The Merseybeats. Bob had already put this to Bill Harry, who owned *The Merseybeat* paper, and he seemed happy with it, although the lads first had to see Bill Harry themselves at his office in Renshaw Street.

Faron was on the show the third week, when they played under the name of The Merseybeats. He came up to the lads after they had done their set saying how much he had enjoyed their playing, which really gave them a boost, as Faron was quite big around Liverpool. The group were beginning to make quite a name for themselves. By this time, The Beatles had already taken off around Merseyside and the rest of the country and The Merseybeats went under Brian Epstein's management, along with The Beatles and The Big Three. The Merseybeats soon got it into their heads that Brian Epstein did not take them seriously enough. He had just had new suits made for The Beatles, and The Merseybeats thought he was not paying them the same attention, and left.

The Merseybeats were still a young group at that time and maybe a little impetuous to jump ship so quickly and they realised later that it had been a bad move to quit the Epstein stable. The group still did well though, having a great mix of songs ranging from The Everleys to The Shirelles and they were still ardent Beatles fans as well. The group went under the management of Kit Lambert, who also managed The Who. The Merseybeats already had a Decca deal, but decided to sign up with Fontana instead. The group had won the contract for Decca at the Philharmonic, but knowing what went on with other groups, in particular, The Beatles having bad experiences with the label, they decided against it. They were lucky enough to be able to choose and opted for Fontana, signing with producer Jack Baberstock from the old school Tin Pan Alley days. They were recording material that they were not completely happy with. As Billy explained, the problem was that they were not writing their own songs. He then quit to start a group of his own, The Kinsleys, but never really got any breaks.

At the end of 1964, Billy rejoined The Merseybeats and the group carried on recording and touring extensively. Kit Lambert then came up with an idea for Tony and Billy to form a duo called The Merseys, a name by which they were already known in the London area. The group disbanded and Aaron Williams decided to quit playing and The Merseys were formed. The only song that received any credit was *Sorrow*, which took them into the charts, reaching number four in April 1966, under the Fontana label. The band's best chart success was with *I Think of You*, which peaked at number five in January 1964.

The Merseybeats' name was later readopted and the band successfully toured, breaking into the cabaret scene. In the mid-seventies Billy formed The Liverpool Express and had some chart success with songs like *You Are My Love*, which went in at number eleven in the charts. One of my favourites was *Every Man Must Have a Dream*, which reached number seventeen in December 1976. In 1989, drummer John Banks, founder member of The Merseybeats, sadly passed away. A memorial show was held in his name and former Liverpool group members turned out to show their respect and out of this came the Merseycats Children's Charity.

The Midnighters

In the late 1950s and early 1960s, Brian Woods was a member of a Skiffle group called The Morrockans. The group were playing Shadows and Skiffle songs of the day, in and around Wirral. As they became more established they began to venture across the Mersey to Liverpool. After a year or so on the club circuit, Brian met up with Gus Travis, with whom he eventually teamed up on bass guitar and vocals. Gus was the instigator in naming the group Gus Travis and the Midnighters. Their line-up was Gus on vocals, Dave Carden on lead guitar, Alan Watts on piano, John Cochrane (also the manager) on drums, Ian Maquair on rhythm guitar and Brian Woods on bass guitar / vocals. The group became popular on Merseyside, playing venues like the Iron Door, the Blue Angel Club, the Cavern and the Plaza in St Helens. They also played The New Brighton Tower.

In 1963, Gus left the group for domestic reasons, later re-emerging on the scene as Gus Travis and the Dymonds. He also joined The Rainchecks, as Gus Travis and the Rainchecks, with whom he stayed till early 1964. Brian says that his talents were greatly missed and left the group without a front man.

Alan, the player manager, was in search of someone who could live up to the standard of The Midnighters. The search came to an end when he came across Freddie Fowell, a singer at a club in Grange Road, Birkenhead. Alan offered him the job and within a week he was practising with The Midnighters on the top floor of the Hoylake Conservative Club.

Freddie fitted in well with the group, although Alan didn't think his surname suited their image and Ian came up with the name Starr. The group also toured the country with The Beatles. Brian's most vivid memory of playing alongside the fab four, was the promotional night for their single *Please Please Me* at the Majestic Ballroom, Birkenhead. The group also appeared at the famous Star Club in Hamburg. Freddie left the group in 1964 and joined the Flamingos, as Freddie Starr and The Flamingos, till the end of 1964. He later joined a cabaret band, Freddie Starr and The Delmonts, with whom he played till 1969.

The Night Boppers

The Night Boppers were originally a Skiffle group, The Pythons, formed by Roy Hilton and Keith Halliwell in the late fifties. After some member changes, original lead vocalist Mark Falcon – who incidentally appeared with Adam Faith at two of his gigs and acted as backing band for him – left the group and Dave Peacock became lead vocalist.

The Night Boppers played the local gigs around Atherton and Manchester. Their line-up was Dave Peacock as lead singer, Eddie Hitchen on bass guitar, Denis Taylor on saxophone, Ray Sale on drums, John Sharples on lead guitar and Jim Anderton on rhythm guitar. Two Liverpool agents who had heard them play introduced them to the Liverpool scene in the early 1960s. They worked with Merseyside groups like The Ravens – who later became Faron's Flamingos – and The Beatles. They also worked alongside one of Liverpool's most outstanding personalities – the disc jockey and compere, Bob Wooler. The Night Boppers played at the Aintree Institute with The Beatles on their farewell show on 28 Feb 1961, before going to Germany. Bob Wooler was impressed with this out-of-town group and, of course, with The Beatles themselves. They were offered work in Germany, but declined. They also played on the same bill as Ian and the Zodiacs at St Luke's in Crosby, or the 'Jive Hive', as it was billed. Ian and The Zodiacs became firm favourites both in Liverpool and Germany and it seems a pity that The Night Boppers split up so soon, as who knows where they might have ended up. They were certainly given good reviews from agent Dave Forshaw.

Dave Peacock informs me that, sadly, Jim Anderton and John Sharples are no longer with us, but are fondly remembered by him and the rest of the group. Dave Peacock was also at the time a semi-pro middle-weight wrestler and one of his opponents was Vic Faulkner from Bolton, who became a professional European middle-weight champion. Dave is also a member of Merseycats.

THE NEWTOWNS

Denis and the Newtowns were a Kirkby-based group, which at that time was a new town on the periphery of Liverpool, hence their name. They played all the local youth dances in the area, including Southdene Hall. The group formed in 1962 and soon built up a big following around

Merseyside, playing clubs like the Iron Door Club, the Mardi Gras Club and the Cavern. The line-up consisted of Glyn Harris on lead guitar, Jimmy Jones on rhythm guitar, Dave Pickstock on bass guitar, Eric Lee on drums and Denis Donafee as lead singer. That line-up remained until 1964, when Dave Pickstock left and Jimmy Jones gave up the rhythm guitar and went on to play bass, Glyn Harris then playing rhythm / lead guitar. The group then took on Bob Fraser on keyboards and started calling themselves The Newtowns. When they played at the Cavern Club it was an all-night session and they were billed alongside chart topping group, The Fortunes. The Newtowns played under that name until they eventually split up in 1967. They never managed to secure a deal with any recording companies but did quite a lot of demo recordings, including an old Spencer Davis number called *Something*, the Judy Garland song *Somewhere Over the Rainbow*, Sandy Shaw's *Tomorrow* and the Drifter's song *Please Stay*, which was also recorded by Liverpool group The Crying Shames, who reached number 26 in the charts.

Denis returned to the music scene many years later with a group called Sandalwood, which was aimed more at the cabaret scene. I had the privilege of playing lead guitar for them for about two years and found Denis to be one of the best vocalists to come out of Liverpool. I remain amazed that he never had any recording deals, despite his tremendous vocal range. The demos recorded by The Newtowns can be heard on a compilation CD, *Unearthed Merseybeat*, on Viper Records.

The Pressmen

This Wallasey-based group started out around 1959 and consisted of Bob Pears on bass guitar / vocals, Richy Prescott on lead guitar, Dave Roberts on rhythm guitar and Nick Arnott on drums. They played the New Brighton, Birkenhead, and Liverpool Rock and Roll scenes. After a time, Nick Arnott decided to leave the group and a drummer by the name of Tommy Bennet replaced him. They were to have an even more dramatic change to their line-up when Phil McKenzie joined the group, he played tenor saxophone and encouraged Dave Roberts to change over to saxophone / guitar. The line-up was quite impressive on stage and they played many Soul classics. Brian Epstein advised the group that they lacked a front man, someone who would liven up the act, but finding the right person was not easy. They finally settled on singer Derry Wilkie, who was previously with The Seniors. He had a lot of experience behind him and was influenced by Ray Charles and Little Richard. Derry and the Seniors were also one of the first groups to play in Germany. The Pressmen then became Derry Wilkie and the Pressmen.

They were one of many groups that recorded for John Schroeder on the album *This is Merseybeat*, recorded live at the Rialto Ballroom. Change came when Tommy Bennet broke away from the group and formed a trio called The New Pressmen. A new drummer was brought in called Aynsley Dunbar. Derry Wilkie and the Pressmen carried on under the same name and brought in Dave Carden, previously with the Midnighters. The group kept that line-up until they finally parted company. Derry and Phil McKenzie formed Derry Wilkie and the Others, and the rest of the group formed The Flamingos. Aynsley Dunbar went on to be one of the most prominent drummers to come out of Liverpool, playing with groups like White Snake and John Mayall's Blues Band. The Pressmen were also a backing group for Cilla Black on Sunday nights at the Kraal Club in Wallasey. Ringo Starr stood in on one number at the hole in the wall stage at the Kraal Club. The Pressmen were one of those groups that other groups would often go to watch perform.

Gerry and the Pacemakers

Gerry Marsden was still in his teens when his first Skiffle group was formed in the late fifties. On drums was his brother Freddie, Jimmy Tobin was on the tea-chest bass, Ken (Dixie) Dean on the washboard and thimbles (Ken later joined a group called the Kruzads), and Gerry on lead vocals / guitar. The lads were all from the Dingle area of Liverpool and even at this early stage in their career, their talent was recognised. George Harrison, who wrote a column in the *Liverpool Echo* called *Over the Mersey Wall*, had spotted the group at a Liverpool charity show, when they were called Gerry Marsden and his Skiffle Group. He wrote, "They impressed me tremendously when I heard them performing. I'll pass a word along. I am sending a few words of recommendation about the boys to our old pal Hughie Green, the television and radio star. He likes to hear of talent like this in unexpected places."

They entered the many Skiffle contests, along with many of their fellow skifflers, such as the Quarry Men. Like most of the groups at that time, the line-up was very fluid and never stayed the same for long. When Skiffle started to fade away, they veered towards Rock and Roll, just as most of the groups did, influenced by people like Elvis Presley, Buddy Holly, Bill Hayley, Gerry Lee Lewis etc. Not only did their style of music change, but also their line-up. Freddie was still on drums, Gerry guitar / vocals, Les Chadwick on bass guitar, and Les McGuire later came in on keyboards, having previously been with the group who eventually became The Undertakers. Gerry's new line-up needed a catchy new name – a name which was to become renowned the world over – Gerry and the Pacemakers.

They were one of Liverpool's top groups, and like most of the Merseybeat groups, they made their way to Hamburg. On one trip they were joined by Faron from the Tempest Tornadoes, a real all-round entertainer, who was later to achieve great acclaim with Faron's Flamingos and The Big Three. The group went under the management of Brian Epstein, who had already taken on The Beatles. Gerry and the Pacemakers had their first record release, a Mitch Murray song, *How Do You Do It?* which reached the number one spot in March 1963, on the Columbia label, with a follow-up, *I Like It*, which also went in at number one. The group reached number one for the third time with *You'll Never Walk Alone*, a song which has since been adopted by Liverpool football supporters. Three number ones in the same year kept the group busy on tour and in the recording studios and they saw further success when they featured in the film, *Ferry Cross the Mersey*, which was filmed on location in Liverpool at such places as the Locarno Ballroom and the Pier Head. Accompanying it was a single, *Ferry Cross the Mersey*, an LP release and an EP, *Hits from Ferry Cross the Mersey*.

The group had done it all. They had toured with The Beatles, made their mark on television and on the American scene, and kept on releasing records. However, they couldn't manage to hit the number one spot again, so in 1965, they decided to call it a day.

Gerry got involved in West End shows and television, although he later formed a new line-up of Pacemakers for the occasional live shows. His best single in my opinion was *Don't Let the Sun Catch You Crying*, which was released in April 64, and went to number six in the charts. They really were a great group and one of the leading lights of the Merseybeat era.

THE QUARRY MEN

PROGRAMME

STALLS — SIDESHOWS — ICE CREAM — LEMONADE

Teas and Refreshments in large Marquee situated behind the hut.

2-00 p.m. PROCESSION leaves Church Road, via Allerton Road, Kings Drive, Hunt's Cross Avenue; returning to the Church Field.
Led by the Band of the Cheshire Yeomanry.
Street Collection by the Youth Club during the procession.

3-00 p.m. CROWNING OF THE ROSE QUEEN (Miss Sally Wright) by Mrs. THELWALL JONES.

3-10 p.m. FANCY DRESS PARADE.
Class 1. Under 7 years.
Class 2. 7 to 12 years.
Class 3. Over 12 years.
Entrants to report to Miss P. Fuller at the Church Hall before the procession.

3-30 p.m. to 5-00 p.m. MUSICAL SELECTIONS by the Band of the Cheshire (Earl of Chester) Yeomanry. Band-master: H. Abraham.
(By permission of Lt.-Col. G. C. V. Churton, M.C., M.B.E.).

4-15 p.m. THE QUARRY MEN SKIFFLE GROUP.

5-15 p.m. DISPLAY by the City of Liverpool Police Dogs. By kind permission of the Chief Constable and Watch Committee.

5-45 p.m. THE QUARRY MEN SKIFFLE GROUP

8-0 p.m. GRAND DANCE in the CHURCH HALL

GEORGE EDWARDS BAND also *The Quarry Men Skiffle Group*

TICKETS 2/-

REFRESHMENTS AT MODERATE PRICES

We now go back to the 1950s and to the Woolton area of Liverpool, where two pupils at Quarry Bank School could hardly let a day go by without getting into some kind of mischief. These two lads were John Winston Lennon and Pete Shotton. John, in particular, was already into the American music scene, Elvis Presley being a major influence. John got his first guitar and picked up a few chords through watching his mother, Julia, who played the banjo. He soon persuaded Pete Shotton to play the washboard, so they could form a Skiffle group. They then brought in Bill Smith to play the tea-chest bass. Eric Griffith was on guitar, Rod Davies on banjo and Colin Hanton on drums. The tea-chest position alternated between Nigel Whalley and Ivan Vaughn but Nigel eventually opted to manage the group rather than play, leaving the mainstay of the tea-chest bass to Len Garry, a good friend of both John and Pete's.

One of their strangest encounters whilst playing was when they set up their equipment on the back of a coal lorry in Rosebery Street. The occasion was the celebration of King John's Royal Charter, on 22 June 1957. The next booking was at St Peter's Church Fete in Church Road, Woolton, on 6 July 1957, where they were to play once again on the back of a lorry, but this time as part of a procession leaving Church Road at 2pm via Allerton Road,

King's Drive, Hunts Cross Avenue and finally arriving back at Church Road. Once there, they set up their equipment again to perform on a makeshift stage at the rear of the church, where the fete was held with the usual sideshows and stalls selling pottery, cakes and homemade jam. The group were to play two sessions in the afternoon, the first at 4.15pm, and the second after the police dog show at 5.45pm. This was the session in which Paul McCartney first encountered John Lennon's Quarry Men, after Ivan Vaughn had invited him to watch them play. At the evening booking at the church hall Paul was introduced to John and the rest of the group as they were setting up their instruments. John had already heard about Paul and his guitar playing, from Ivan, and before long Paul was displaying both his guitar and vocal talents playing his rendition of *Twenty Flight Rock*. The Quarry Men played two sets that evening, along with The George Edwards Band. Within a couple of weeks, after some discussion, Paul McCartney became a member of The Quarry Men. His presence made a noticeable difference to the group; his vocals, in particular, but also his influence in teaching John some new guitar chords.

The Quarry Men's style was unique, as was their sound, with more and more American influenced Rock and Roll songs such as *Lucille* and *Long Tall Sally* – both covers of Little Richard songs – and performed by Paul. The group carried on with the same line-up, with the addition of John Lowe, the pianist, standing in on the odd occasion when the club or hall had a piano. August of 1958 saw the sudden illness of the tea-chest bass player, Len Garry, who ended up in Fazakerley Hospital diagnosed with meningitis. Len spent seven months recovering in hospital, as The Quarry Men carried on with their music.

They were soon to recruit a new member to the group, George Harrison, an acquaintance of Paul McCartney's, who was a bit younger than the other lads but could play a mean guitar. His main influences were Rock and Roll, Carl Perkins style. A friend of George's, Ken Brown, also joined the group but only for a short spell. Like many other Liverpool groups, they paid a visit to Phillips Recording Studio, which was set up in an old house in Kensington and made an acetate of Buddy Holly's *That'll Be the Day* and a Harrison / McCartney song, *In Spite of All the Danger*. Another new member was Stuart Sutcliffe, an art college friend of John Lennon's, who reluctantly joined the group as bass player. It was Sutcliffe who brought an end to the name The Quarry Men and introduced The Beatles, with the emphasis on the 'beat'. And so The Beatles were born.

Cliff Roberts and the Rockers

Allan Schroeder started out in the music scene with a group called The Cravats. He then joined up with his brother Dave, Cliff Roberts, Roy McAllister and Malcolm Linnell. Incidentally, Allan's brother had made one of the first bass guitars in Wirral, by doubling up each of the four guitar strings to achieve that deep, bass sound.

Their first gig, at Hollyoake Hall, was arranged by Bob Evans, who was with The Five Shillings. The bookings then escalated and the band played at the Grosvenor Ballroom, Blair Hall and many other top Merseyside venues. An event that stands out for Allan, was when the group auditioned for Larry Parnes, who was looking for a backing group for Billy Fury. The audition was held at the Wyvern Club, in Seel Street, on 10 May 1960.

The Silver Beetles were also at the audition, along with Gerry Marsden and his group. Larry Parnes dismissed them, informing Cliff Roberts that they were not looking for another Cliff Richard. Cliff Roberts and the Rockers finally found themselves as the resident group at the Temple Bar, but the strain of all the commuting backwards and forwards to the club from the other side of the Mersey put pressure on the group. Missing the last bus or ferry home didn't help either and the group disbanded at the end of this residency. They were one of many great groups to emerge from the other side of the Mersey. Allan still plays today, putting on shows for Merseycats and is still an excellent drummer. The members of the group in the photograph are, from left to right, Cliff Roberts on vocals, Malcolm Linnell on bass guitar, Dave Myers on lead guitar, Kenny (Nipper) Johnson on rhythm guitar and in the foreground, on drums, Allan Schroeder. The picture was taken around 1961.

The Remo Four

We now go back to 1958, when the Remo Quartet first came on to the music scene. The line-up was Don Andrew on bass guitar / vocals, Keith Stokes on guitar / vocals, Colin Manley on lead guitar and Harry Prytherch on drums. They worked for most of the local promoters, like Charlie McBain – who did the bookings for Wilson Hall, as well as Brian Kelly, Dave Forshaw and Sam Leach. May 1961 saw a name change from The Remo Quartet to the Remo Four. They were getting more and more work, as well as acquiring a big following. Among their fans was Paul McCartney, who considered Colin Manley to be one of the finest guitarists around Liverpool at the time. The group played at the Cavern as guests of the Swinging Blue Jeans, of whom they were big fans and also appeared alongside The Shadows, who were their role models. On this occasion Hank Marvin commented that The Remo was the better group on that particular gig! The Remo Four were also on the same bill as The Beatles on their very first evening appearance at the Cavern and actually played on the same bill as The Beatles for about forty different gigs.

In 1962, Harry Prytherch decided to quit the scene for a while, as the group at that time was one of the hardest working on Merseyside. Harry was not out of the group scene for long, however, as a new group was about to emerge, Group One, with Keith Stokes from the Remo Four on guitar / vocals, Harry Prytherch on drums, Dave Williams (previously with Dale Roberts and the Jaywalkers) on lead guitar / vocals and Eric London (formerly with Faron's Flamingos) on bass guitar. Group One was one of the groups featured in the BBC documentary, *The Mersey Sound*, along with The Beatles. They also appeared on the same bill as the Rolling Stones, at the Locarno Ballroom, in Liverpool. The Remo Four then took on Roy Dyke, who replaced Harry on drums and Phil Rogers replaced Keith Stokes on guitar. The Remo went on to tour the American bases in France. They backed Johnny Sandon, who was previously with The Searchers, and they also went on to back Tommy Quickly, under the Epstein management.

Over the years, the group were often called upon as a backing group, although they could have made it on their own merit, as they were an excellent harmony group. Tony Ashton was introduced into the group and Colin decided it was time to leave, later joining the Swinging Blue Jeans and touring with them in Europe and England. What was left of the Remo Four joined up with a guy called Gardener and formed Ashton, Gardener and Dyke who had a hit with *The Resurrection Shuffle*. The Remo Four were another of Liverpool's finest instrumental vocal groups, probably at their best playing Shadows material.

Solomon's Mines

Before joining Solomon's Mines, Tom Flude was with a schoolboy group at the age of thirteen or fourteen. The lads used to practise at a bingo hall, but since they didn't own a set of drums, one of them used a set of bongos given to him by his brother who was away at sea. The manager of the hall said he would buy a second-hand set for the group, on the understanding that they played during the intermission. He kept his word and took the lads down to a music shop and bought them a set of drums. One day, after school, the group made their way down to the bingo hall to practise, only to find a policeman taking the manager away. After a quick discussion, it was decided that they had better grab their drum kit and go home, in case it was taken off them. As they had still not found a name for themselves, they decided to call the group after the manager, Mr Dean; hence the name The Deans.

Tom's father then took over the group's bookings and one day he came home with their first booking at the Cavern Club, on a Saturday afternoon, having acquired it through Bob Wooler. Also performing were The Escorts and The Kirkbys. The group later auditioned at the Adelphi Hotel for the film *Ferry Cross the Mersey,* starring Gerry Marsden. The lads were asked if they could get three days off school for rehearsals at the Locarno. They were over the moon at the thought of being in the film, but to their disappointment they were overlooked and a group called The Blackwells were brought in instead. By way of compensation, Gerry arranged for them to be extras in the film.

Soon afterwards, Tom quit the band for a while, until a couple of the lads from Solomon's Mines asked him to join them on keyboards, along with two other members of The Deans. Solomon's Mines, who at that time were only about sixteen years of age, made it through to the first stage of the finals of Search for Sound, which was run through the Silver Blades Ice Rink in Shiel Road, Liverpool. It took place on a Friday night and was aimed at semi-professional groups. It went on for a couple of months. The competition worked on a ballot system, the audience voting for their favourite group. They were up against five or six groups and got through to the semi-finals in Manchester and then on to the finals at Streatham Ice Rink, London. The coveted prize was a recording contract. The winners were a group called Mud, who later had hits with songs such as, *Tiger Feet* and *Lonely This Christmas*. From that point on, the bookings for Solomon's Mines started to decrease and the group finally disbanded around 1968.

The Swinging Blue Jeans

The group originally started out in the late fifties as The Blue Genes, specialising in Jazz and Skiffle, with the main thrust of the group being Jazz. Ray Ennis was on guitar / vocals, Norman Kuhlke was on washboard, but later moved over to drums, Bruce McCaskill was on guitar / vocals, Spud Ward was on double bass, but later teamed up with Rory Storm's group, The Raving Texans and was replaced by James Hudson. Tommy Hughes was the banjo player and came from The Pinetop Skiffle Group. The group was still playing Jazz, as it still had a strong following in Liverpool. Soon afterwards, Ralph Ellis joined the group on guitar / vocals and Les Braid took over the double bass from Jimmy Hudson. The group were still playing places like the Cavern when Tommy Hughes left to do his National Service and was replaced by Paul Moss. Bruce was later to leave and form a group called the Kansas City Five. Some time later, Tommy met Bruce at the Mardi-Gras Club in Liverpool and shortly after that meeting became a member of the Kansas City Five. Bruce later worked as a roadie and ended up with Eric Clapton, from whom he acquired a car for his services! From the proceeds of the sale of the car he had enough money to take a group called the Average White Band to fame and fortune. The Blue Genes had been quite successful at the Cavern, holding special guest nights and inviting along groups like The Beatles.

The group finally answered the call to Germany and headed for the Star Club in Hamburg, in 1962. However, they had to undergo a drastic change to their style of music in order to satisfy their German audiences, and played some foot-tapping Rock and Roll standards. They came back to Liverpool quite transformed and thought it was time to get into the recording side of the business, quite unaware of the success that lay ahead of them. They ended up with a string of records in the charts such as, *It's Too Late Now*, which they had out in June 1963. Their follow up record, *Hippy Hippy Shake*, came out in December that same year; a song they will fondly remember, as it carried on having chart success right into 1964.

As a four-piece group, they became household names enjoying world-wide acclaim. In 1966, the group had another chart hit with the memorable, *Don't Make Me Over*, which must rate as one of their best. Today they are as busy as ever touring, but can always find time to do charity work for people like Merseycats, and other organisations. Colin Manley, who had previously played with The Remo Four, eventually took over lead guitar. He played with the group from 1978 till 1999, when he sadly passed away - he was one of the best Rock and Roll guitarists around. Les Braid, the long-standing bass guitarist with group, also sadly passed away in 2005.

THE SEARCHERS

It is hard to believe that The Searchers slipped through Brian Epstein's net, yet they did; a great loss on his part. Instead, the group went under the management of Les Ackerley, who, as most of the Merseybeat musicians will remember, was involved with the Iron Door Club, at Number 13 Temple Street, Liverpool. John McNally and Mike Pender both started out in the Skiffle days. The lads later formed a group with Tony Jackson, and were also joined by drummer Chris Crummy, who eventually changed his name to Chris Curtis. The group later brought in vocalist Bill Beck, who went under the stage name of Johnny Sandon. The group started to attract a lot of recognition, especially at places like the Cavern, playing alongside such groups as The Beatles and Gerry and the Pacemakers, on the Blue Jeans guest nights. Johnny stayed with the group until February 1962 and his last booking with The Searchers at the Cavern would have been 23 February 1962. Johnny then joined The Remo Four and travelled to France to play the American bases. I played the bases myself, a great training ground for any group, especially with a group like The Remo Four behind you, as my good friend Harry Prytherch would tell you, as he played drums with them in the early Remo Four days.

Meanwhile, the Searchers decided to stay as a four-piece group. In October 1962 they followed the path of other Liverpool groups and signed up to play at the Star Club in Hamburg. Their music was very well received, earning them a return booking in February 1963, on the same bill as Ray Charles. The group later made a demo recording, with which their manager approached PYE records. They were accepted and signed up. Their first single was *Sweets for My Sweet*, which was released in June 1963. At the time of release the group were back in Hamburg. To their great surprise, they made the number one position on 27 June 1963, and stayed in the charts for 16 weeks. They made the top ten charts again with *Sugar and Spice*, which reached number two on 24 Oct 1963 and stayed in the charts for 13 weeks. The song was written by the man who looked after their recordings at PYE, Tony Hatch and he also looked after fellow Liverpool group, The Undertakers. The Searchers had a second number one with *Needles and Pins* in January 1964. Then on 16 April 1964, they achieved their third number one with *Don't Throw Your Love Away*. This was to be their last British number one single, although they carried on having chart releases.

Tony Jackson then decided to quit The Searchers and formed a group called Tony Jackson and the Vibrations, which hit the charts with a single on 8 October 1964, *Bye Bye Baby / Watch Your Step*, on the PYE label, reaching number 38. Tony's replacement was bass guitarist Frank Allan. I know many musicians will remember him from The Rebel Rousers, who had hits with *One Way Love*, in 1964, *I'll Take You Home*, in 1965, and *Got to Get You into My Life*, in 1966, reaching number six in the charts. I last saw The Rebel Rousers playing live for Merseycats – still a brilliant band!

Chris Curtis, drummer with the group, also decided to leave The Searchers and was replaced by John Blunt. The Searchers carried on into the mid-eighties, when Mike Pender broke away from the group and formed Mike Pender's Searchers. The Searchers are still one of my favourite groups and you can still see one of The Searchers groups playing today. Sadly, Chris Curtis has recently passed away.

Denny Seyton and the Sabres

In an interview with Bernie Rogers, the drummer with numerous groups from Liverpool, we go back to 1958, and the Skiffle era, to a group called The Moon Rockers. The group consisted of Geoff Hughes on rhythm guitar, Kevin Kennedy, John Kirkpatrick and, at that time, Bernie on washboard / guitar. They played all the cover songs of the late fifties, until the end of 1959, when they changed their name to The Travellers. The Skiffle sound was on the wane and electric instruments had started to replace the acoustic guitars. Geoff Hughes decided to leave the group and so Freddie Ennis stepped in on bass guitar, joining Eddie Houlihan on rhythm guitar, John Kirkpatrick on lead guitar and Bernie on drums. With a vocalist called John, they became Johnny Saint and the Travellers. The group played the local circuit, in places like Blair Hall and the David Lewis Theatre, until the end of 1961. A well-known character in Liverpool, Joe Flannery, was putting together a new group to back his brother Lee Curtis, and took Bernie on to play drums. Wayne Bickerton was on bass guitar / vocals, Tony Waddington on rhythm guitar / vocals and Frank Bowen on lead guitar. The group became very well known on the Merseybeat scene.

Bernie had been promised the job of drummer, once there was an opening, with Denny Seyton and the Sabres, who had a recording deal in the pipeline. Before joining the Sabres, Bernie stepped in with The

Memphis Three with Brendan McCormack for a few months. Lee Curtis and the All Stars went on to record for the Decca label. Wayne Bickerton and Tony Waddington went to State Records, with hits by The Rubettes and Mac and Katie Kissoon.

Denny Seyton and the Sabres recorded on the Mercury label, also releasing an LP on the Wing label, a sister company for American releases. Ian and the Zodiacs also recorded a twelve track LP for the same label. Denny Seyton and the Sabres' version of fourteen cover songs called, *It's the Gear,* was released in March 1965. Three singles were released for the Mercury label: *Tricky Dicky / Baby What You Want Me to Do*, in February 1964, followed by *Short Fat Fannie / Give Me Back My Heart* in June 1964, and then, in September 1964, *The Way You Look Tonight / Hands Off*. There was another release as the Denny Seyton Group, recorded for Parlophone in late 1965, *Just a Kiss / In the Flowers by the Trees.*

Bernie played with Denny Seyton and the Sabres until about 1965, when he moved to London to work as session drummer for the Mercury label, which was at that time run by Tom Spingfield. Bernie worked with most of the top stars in London, including Matt Monroe, Ben E King and Dusty Springfield on shows like *Ready Steady Go*. Bernie returned to Liverpool around 1971 and later joined up with Faron's Flamingos, who put on many shows for Merseycats; a much appreciated and extremely talented musician and events organiser. Geoff Hughes made a career for himself as an actor, best known for his part as Eddie Yates in *Coronation Street*.

Track listings on *It's the Gear: Hippy Hippy Shake, Needles and Pins, Candy Man, All My Loving, Good Golly Miss Molly, Little Children, I Want to Hold Your Hand, Bits and Pieces, I Think of You, Can't Buy Me Love, Just One Look, Not Fade Away, I'm the One and Glad All Over.*

Billy Butler and the Tuxedos

The first time I stepped out on to the same stage as Billy, was when he was a disc jockey at the Cavern Club. Around that time, 1967, I was playing guitar for a group called Tyme and Motion, but Billy had been on the scene long before that, due to his involvement in the Thank Your Lucky Stars television show, on which he was a member of the panel. On one occasion, George Harrison asked Billy if he could give The Beatles a plug the next time he appeared on the show, but he had to decline, saying he had been working with The Merseybeats and felt it would not be fair to them.

Billy remembers his time spent working with the Merseybeats as surprise singer, when they used to have a special guest night at St Johns, in Bootle, and for the first couple of songs he wore a mask. On one occasion the Merseybeats chose The Beatles as their guest group of the week. Billy originally started out with a group called The Hangmen, but was better known for his group Billy Butler and the Tuxedos. Their line-up was Billy on vocals, Les Williams on lead guitar – who also played for The Dimensions, John O'Brien on guitar, Al Crowley on bass guitar and Ronnie Myers on drums, later to be replaced by Reg Coulsting. Billy became more and more involved in being a disc jockey and compere, working in the Cavern and other clubs around Liverpool and has ended up hosting his own radio spot for a BBC radio station in Liverpool. He does occasionally reform The Tuxedos for the odd show. Billy is also involved with quite a few different charity organisations, such as the Variety Club, Give a Child a Chance and Merseycats. Billy Butler and the Tuxedos have recorded on The Class of 64 CDs, distributed through Radio Merseyside's disc jockey, Frankie Connor.

Tyme and Motion

The group originally started as Rita and the Rebs, around 1965, with Rita Jacobson on vocals, Richy Conner on drums, Roy Ennis also on vocals, Ray Bright on guitar / vocals and John Ross on bass. The line-up changed around mid-1966, coinciding with the change of name to Tyme and Motion. Roy Ennis and Ray Bright were still on vocals and John Ross on bass, but Bobby Ninnim was brought in as the new drummer, as well as Tony Petches on lead guitar and Allan Luckett on rhythm guitar. The group played the local youth dances such as St Luke's and the Star of the Sea. They played throughout 1966 together, until the line-up changed again when Bobby Ninnim sadly died. Bobby Milne, who had just filled his position, had just left The Admins, who were a Kirkby based group.

Tyme and Motion were a harmony group with Beach Boys style vocals from Ray and Roy, who this time were both out front singers. Their style came across strongly on a demo recording they did of *September in the Rain* and *Kelly* – a Del Shannon classic. The group were to have another change in the line-up when Tony left. Alan then stepped in on lead guitar and Ray went back on to rhythm guitar. Nothing then changed until Eric Woolley joined the group as rhythm guitarist, via Alan Luckett, with whom I had played guitar some years before. Ray then went out front again with Roy, minus Ray's guitar! The line-up stayed the same throughout the remainder of 1967, then, in 1968, Ray decided to leave. The vocals were then taken on by Roy and John Ross, who both had excellent voices.

Tyme and Motion made their way to London to record a demo for a studio called Cavern Studios. Unfortunately, nothing came of it and the group returned to Liverpool to play all their old haunts such as the Cavern, Litherland Town Hall and Orrell Park Ballroom, workeing mainly for Dave Forshaw. They decided to call it a day in 1969, but reformed again in 1984 with Ray Bright on vocals, Alan Luckett on guitar, Dave Smith on lead guitar, John Ross on bass and Chris Mutch on drums. By the end of 1969, Bobby Milne and Eric Woolley were playing in Germany with a group called The Almost Young. Ray Ennis has sadly passed away.

The Undertakers

The Undertakers were a Wallasey based group, their name the result of a mistake in the print room of the *Liverpool Echo*, where, instead of The Vegas Five, they were advertised as The Undertakers. The line-up was Bob Evens on drums, Geoff Nugent on rhythm guitar, Chris Huston on lead guitar / vocals, Mushy Cooper on bass, Jimmy McManus on vocals and Brian Jones on saxophone. The line-up soon changed when Bob left the group and Bugs Pemberton was recruited as their new drummer. The group underwent another change of personnel when Mushy Cooper left the group and was replaced by Jackie Lomax, who added some excellent vocals to their sound. Mushy later teamed up with Faron's Flamingos. Jimmy McManus also left and joined a group called The Renegades. The group was managed by Ralph Webster, who is remembered for his association with the Orrell Park Ballroom. He also managed Ian and The Zodiacs.

The Undertakers were recognised by their trademark outfits of long black drape coats, styled on the American tombstone days, when undertakers wore black matching hats. The group not only looked the part but also had a solid and exciting Rock and Roll sound. They finally found their way to Germany for a nine-week gig at the Star Club in Hamburg, the first of many, as the group eventually notched up over 140 appearances there. The Undertakers were one of the hardest working groups on Merseyside, with television work and a recording deal with PYE. They were overseen by Tony Hatch, but they could never agree over record releases. Their first single was *Everybody Loves a Lover* with the flip side *Mashed Potato* – a song everyone recognises as an Undertakers' song, although it was actually originally a Rozier song, released in 1963. A second single followed that same year entitled *What About Us / Money*. The group went from strength to strength and early 1964 saw another release, *Just a Little Bit / Stupidity*. *Stupidity* was also covered by another Merseybeat group, Kingsize Taylor and the Dominoes. They were to have another release under the shortened name of The Takers, an idea put forward by PYE, who saw the name The Undertakers as potentially distasteful. But the group were dissatisfied and The Undertakers finally parted company with the PYE label, who had not pushed them as far as they could have.

The group eventually answered an advertisement for a working British band to go to New York, but once again they were misrepresented and the group had to commute to Canada for bookings. The only good thing to come out of the American trip was an LP recorded at Talent Masters Studio, New York. Jackie Lomax also got a record deal with Apple records in 1968, and Chris decided to stay in America, as a sound engineer for Talent Master. The American LP is now out on CD, having just been re-released after all these years. The Undertakers were an excellent Merseybeat group.

Geoff Nugent is now a member of the Merseycats children's charity.

The Viscounts

Bill Jones, an avid Lonnie Donegan fan, purchased his double bass from Jim Gretty, who was a salesman and also a well-known character in Frank Hessy's music shop in Liverpool. The bass cost the staggering sum of £82, which in those days was a small fortune, so it was bought on hire purchase at a pound a week. Bill then joined The Viscounts, a group that were popular around the Wallasey area. The line-up was Jock McCabe on drums and his wife Jean on vocals, in the style of Nancy Whiskey, Dave Regine on guitar / vocals, Jimmy Turpin on lead guitar / vocals and Bill Jones on bass. The group entered and won a heat of the Carrol Levis Show, held at the Pavilion Theatre in Lodge Lane, Liverpool. The groups only played one number each, so The Viscounts put a lot a rehearsing into the Jimmy Rogers' song, *Honeycomb*. However, unknown to them, another group had picked the same song. So, at the very last minute, they decided to play a Lonnie Donegan favourite, *Rock Island Line*, in the second heat. The competition was judged by audience appreciation and The Viscounts claim that the group that won had packed the place with family and friends.

In Brighton Street, Seacombe, there was a disused hall called the Star Ballroom. The Viscounts took it over for three nights a week, bringing other groups in to play on a percentage of the door takings. Some of the groups that played there were: The Demons, The Kingpins, The Druids Jazz Band and The Down Town Boys. Arrangements were made for female volunteers to sell soft drinks and crisps in the interval, when the 78s would go on the record player, while the musicians slipped out for a pint at the Brighton Hotel. When the group eventually disbanded, Billy went with The Billy Jay Combo, taking resident work at the West Indian clubs such as Dutch Eddie's and the International. And to think it all started with tea-chest bass and washboard!

Ian and the Zodiacs

The group started out as a Jazz band, in 1958, playing around the Crosby and Seaforth area. Dave Lovelady was on drums with Pete Pimlett on guitar, Pete Griffiths on lead guitar and piano, which was also covered by a few players, one of them being Dave Bresnen. The group's format took on a different direction when John Kennedy, a singer / guitarist, joined the line-up. It was was from that point on that their music started getting noticed. The sound was to take on another change, as were the vocals, when Ian Edwards came into the group. Eventually, they became Ian and the Zodiacs and went under the wing of manager Ralph Webster, who also managed the Orrell Park Ballroom and two other ballrooms, which meant the group could always rely on a booking in at least one of the venues. They began to build up a large and enthusiastic following in and around the Liverpool scene, going through quite a few line-up changes. Despite these changes, they always maintained a good sound, as can be heard on *This is Merseybeat*, recorded by John Schroeder on the Oriole label.

Along with many of the Liverpool squadron of Merseybeat groups, they eventually succumbed to the lure of Germany and headed for Hamburg, where the German audiences couldn't get enough of the Liverpool groups and took to them immediately. They recorded for both Fontana and the Wings label, for which they recorded a twelve-track album called *Gear Again* and numerous others over in Germany, where the group eventually settled for quite a few years, until Ian's wife fell ill and they moved back to Liverpool.

Ian eventually teamed up with the Fourmost for a while. In a conversation with manager Ralph Webster, he singled Ian out as one of the finest singers to come out of Liverpool, commenting on the tremendous range and quality of his voice. Ian Edwards is now a member of Merseycats and not too long ago I saw him on the bill of a show called Merseybeat and Laughter and I wholeheartedly agree with Ralph Webster, he still had that special quality to his voice, but since then he has sadly died.

Track listings on *Gear Again:* Eight Days a Week, It's All Over Now, The Rise and Fall of Fingel Bunt, We're Through, Tired of Waiting for You, I Feel Fine, All Day and All of the Night, Game of Love, When You Walk in the Room, Um, um, um, um, um, um, A Hard Day's Night and Silhouettes.

WHO ARE MERSEYCATS?

Original Merseybeat Groups of the Sixties
The Rock and Roll Children's Charity

The inspiration for Merseycats came at a memorial show for the late John Banks, ex-drummer with The Merseybeats, held at the Montrose Club, in 1989. Many of the ex-Merseyside beat groups turned out to show their support for John and, although it was a sad occasion, it rekindled old friendships amongst them. Another reunion of about forty group members was held that same year at the Penny Lane Wine Bar. A decision was made to reform some of the Merseybeat groups, in order to put on shows and raise money for the benefit of the children of Merseyside. Merseycats was formed and a group membership badge was designed called Ambrose Mogg, now worn by Merseyside musicians with pride. The inspiration for this wonderful organisation, which has raised over £250,000 for charity, came from groups like The Fourmost, The Swinging Blue Jeans, Karl Terry and the Cruisers, The Remo Four, Faron's Flamingos, Johnny Guitar and the Hurricanes, The Dominoes, The Undertakers and Earl Preston's TTs.

In 1989, Merseycats raised £12,000 for the NSPCC appeal, KIND, by organising 60s shows at the Philharmonic Hall, Grafton Ballroom and even as far away as Stockport. In 1990, the members voted to support Alder Hey Children's Hospital's 75th birthday appeal. With the help of Radio Merseyside and *the Liverpool Echo*, Merseycats raised a staggering £27,000, one of the largest contributions donated to the appeal. In 1991, Merseycats members gave their services to the Variety Club of Great Britain, raising funds for Sunshine coaches. The vehicles were presented around Merseyside to Meadowbank Special School, Fazakerley, Foxfield School in Moreton and Parkfield School in Kirkby, following a successful show held at Liverpool Empire, held in memory of James Bulger. The Merseycats have also raised money for Strawberry Fields and Claire House.

A Bob Wooler SHOW
TOWER
BALLROOM NEW BRIGHTON
NUMBER ONE ... STAR SHOW
LICENSED BARS
THE BEATLES
Parlophone Recording Artistes
HEY! BABY
BRUCE Channel
AND
DELBERT McLINTON
(HARMONICA)
DIRECT from AMERICA!
WITH The BARONS
THE BIG THREE
THE Statesmen
The NORTH'S FABULOUS FIVE!
THE FOUR JAYS
THURSDAY 21ST JUNE · 1962
7·30 TO 12 P.M.
TICKETS
4'6 IN ADVANCE 5'6 ON THE NIGHT
AVAILABLE FROM
NEMS · RUSHWORTHS · LEWIS'S · HESSYS
STROTHERS Etc. & TOWER BALLROOM

Where Are They Now?

Billy Butler – Tuxedos. Billy moved out of group work and dedicated his time to a career as a disc jockey. He can often be found at record fairs and now works for Radio Merseyside. Billy also does a lot of local charity work.

Joe Butler – The Cascades. Joe went into the country scene with The Hillsiders. When he retired from playing he ran an entertainments agency, and also worked for a local radio playing country sounds. Sadly, Joe recently passed away.

John Byrne – Rory Storm and the Hurricanes. John was involved with the Merseycats, putting on shows around Liverpool to raise money for the children of Merseyside. During the day, he also worked for the Ambulance Service. Sadly, John passed away in 1999.

Frankie Connor – The Hideaways. Frankie retired from the group scene and made a career as a disc jockey, with his own Merseybeat radio show on Radio Merseyside. Frankie also writes songs for many of the Merseyside artists and gives up a lot of his time to charity organisations. Keep on Rocking, Frankie!

Mike Evans – The Clayton Squares. Mike joined the Liverpool scene with Adrian Henri for a few years, but now lives in London and works in the publishing business – another great saxophone player from Merseyside.

Ian Edwards – The Zodiacs. Ian was a successful businessman and was also involved with Merseycats and fundraising. He set up home in Germany for many years but came back to England. He sounded as good as ever until his recent death.

Faron – The Flamingos. Faron spent some time in Germany with Gerry Marsden and the Pacemakers and was bass player for The Big Three. He lived in France, where he had previously entertained the American forces. He formed his own band out there for a while, but now lives back in Liverpool and is also a Merseycat.

Len Garry – The Quarry Men. Len still gets involved with The Beatles convention and also works with the original Quarry Men. He still has a day job working with disabled children. Len has just had his first book published entitled, *John Paul and Me – Before The Beatles*.

Brian Jones – The Undertakers. Brian is one of the finest saxophone players around. He has played with some great groups, including spending a lot of time with The Glitter Band. He still stands in with the local groups, raising money for local charities.

Kenny Johnson – The Cascades. Kenny was also part of one of the finest country groups in England – The Hillsiders and later formed The Northwind. Kenny also hosts his own country spot on Radio Merseyside and helps raise money around Liverpool in charity shows.

Stan Johnson – The Hy-Tones. Stan retired from playing with his group and made a career for himself as a seaman. He later settled down ashore as a taxi driver. Stan recently rekindled some old friendships, when he became a member of Merseycats.

Dave Kent – The Connoisseurs. Dave lives in the Southport area and put lots of hard work into Merseycats as the charity's secretary. He was part of one of the groups that made it both as artists and songwriters.

Billy Kinsley – The Merseybeats. Billy left the group for a while and formed The Liverpool Express, which had some recordings: *You Are My Love* and *Every Man Must Have a Dream*. He is also an excellent songwriter. He can now be found touring again with The Merseybeats.

Judd Lander – The Hideaways. Judd joined a group called Cellophane and move to London, where he is now a freelance musician. He worked with people like Paul McCartney, John Lennon and Albert Hammond.

John Lomax – The Atlantics. John is now a member of The Cheshire Cats and was in charge of filming the sixties groups for Merseycats for quite some time. The group re-forms every now and again to raise money for charity.

Eric London – Group One. Prior to working with Group One, Eric had played bass guitar for Faron's Flamingos. After leaving Group One he retired from the music scene for almost thirty years, but I am glad to say that he's back playing for Merseycats.

Geoff Nugent – The Undertakers. Involved in raising money for Merseycats, as a one-time member of the board, Geoff worked during the day as a site manager for a school in Kirkby, Liverpool. He has now retired but is still a member of Merseycats.

Jimmy O'Connor – The Hy-Tones. He was the rhythm guitar / vocalist with the group and there was a great quality to his voice and it's a shame that he never broke through into the recording side of the business. Later Jimmy joined a barbershop group and more recently became a member of Merseycats.

Dave Peacock – The Night Boppers. Dave was always interested in boxing from an early age and also wrestled semi-professionally, fighting opponents like Vic Faulkner. He gave up group work and was employed by the local authority for many years. He has now retired, but is still a member of Merseycats.

Harry Prytherch – The Remo Four. Harry went into the cabaret scene backing different stars like Frankie Vaughan. He works hard at a day care centre and is also involved with Merseycats in his spare time. He also narrated a show called *The True Story of Merseybeat* with a group called The Copycats.

Bernie Rogers – Denny Seyton and the Sabres. Bernie moved to London to work as a session drummer, working with people like Ben E King and Dusty Springfield. He was involved in putting together shows for Merseycats and put a lot of time in behind the scenes. He still lives in Liverpool.

Bob Scott – The Clayton Squares. Bob works with autistic children organising rock climbing and hill walks. He left the group and worked as resident club drummer for a few years. Now retired from the scene, he dedicates his time to his career.

Wally Shepard – The Tempest Tornadoes. Wally started out with the original Johnny Tempest and the Tempest Tornadoes, who later became Earl Preston and the TTs. Wally is now is on the board of Merseycats.

Kingsize Taylor – The Dominoes. Kingsize has been retired from the music scene for quite some time and is now living in the Southport area, working as a butcher, but he left behind many memorable recordings. Kingsize Taylor and the Dominoes were one of Gerry Marsden's favourite groups. Kingsize has recently reformed with the Dominoes for charity shows.

Karl Terry – The Cruisers. Karl still lives in Liverpool. He works in the building trade during the day but he still finds time to raise money for Merseycats. He is one of the finest Rock and Roll entertainers to come out of Liverpool.

Albie Wycherly – The Centremen. Albie was involved with the Billy Fury fan club, along with his mother Jean Wycherly, putting on shows and raising money for The Billy Fury memorial statue to be made and erected in Liverpool.

Ozzie Yue – The Hideways. Ozzie still does the Liverpool circuit and is an excellent guitarist. He left the Hideaways to join Edwin Starr's band. He later went into acting and can quite often be seen on television. He takes his acting career very seriously.

Saturday Night at the Orrell Park Ballroom

Ralph Webster's Years (1960-63)

Ralph managed the Orrell Park Ballroom, or the OPB, as it was known to the musicians in the sixties, booking the Merseybeat groups there from 1960 to 1963. He also managed Ian and the Zodiacs, Mark Peters and the Silhouettes and The Undertakers. He had another club, the Click Click Club, and also the Heaven and Hell Club in Warrington, with Brian Kelly, who was a well-known promoter around Merseyside. In a telephone conversation with Ralph, he was able to reel off the names of all the groups who appeared at the OPB from 1960 onwards. In his estimation, Ian Edwards was one of the best vocalists to come out of Liverpool at that time. Sadly, not long after my interview with Ralph, I was informed by Geoff Nugent, from the original Undertakers, that Ralph had passed away. Below is a list of most of the bands which appeared at the OPB.

January 1960 – The Silhouettes appeared at the club and won a Skiffle group contest on 18 January1960.

February 1960 – The Skylarks, The Metronomes, The Ravens, The Tornadoes, Johnny and the Jets and Johnny Tempest.

9 May 1960 – Gerry Marsden (who appeared in the interval for £3), The Skyliners, The Deltones, Bobby Bell Rockers and Bobby and the Cadillacs.

8 August 1960 – The Dominoes, who were also paid £3.

26 September 1960 – The Dynamites, The White Brothers and The Asteroids.

27 February 1961 – Rory Storm and The Hurricanes, Frank Knight and the Barrons, Johnny Rocco and Dee Fenton.

20 March 1961 – Faron and the Tempest Tornadoes, Terry and the Tuxedos, Ray and the Delrenas, Dale Roberts and the Jay Walkers, Cliff Roberts' Rockers and Clay Ellis and the Raiders.

24 April 1961 – The Remo Four, Steve and the Syndicate and The Jokers.

14 May 1961 – Ian and the Zodiacs, The Creoles, Danny and the Asteroids, The G-Men and The Galvanisers.

1 July 1961 – The Undertakers.

31 July 1961 – The Strangers, with Joe Fagan in the line-up. Joe made it as a songwriter with *That's Living All Right* and *As Time Goes By*.

26 August 1961 – The Big Three, The Renegades, The Four Jays, The Undertakers and Danny Havoc and the Hi-Cats.

7 October 1961 – Karl Terry and the Cruisers, Vince Wade and the Statesmen and The Climbers.

28 October 1961 – Ken Dallis and the Silhouettes, Steve Bennet and the Syndicate, The Quiet Ones, Johnny Byrne and the Renegades, Liam and the Invaders and Steve Day and the Drifters.

December 1961 – Mark Peters and the Cyclone, Lee Eddie Five, The Martinis, Johnny Sandon and the Searchers, The Travellers, The Satellites, Gus and the Thundercaps, Johnny and the D-Jays and The Zeros.

9 March 1962 – The Dennisons.

April 1962 – Group One, Albie and the Sorrals, The Flintstones and Billy Kramer and the Coasters.

September 1962 – The Kansas City Five.

November 1962 – The Searchers.

16 December 1962 – The Remo Four with Johnny Sandon, The Cimarrons.

1963 – Ricky Gleason and the Top Spots, The Tallboys, Earl Preston and the TTs, The Four Clefs, Lee Shondel and the Boys, Sonny Webb and the Cascades and The Chessmen.

May 1963 – The Fourmost, Vince Earl and the Talismen, Gus Travis and The Rainchecks and Mark Peters and the Silhouettes.

June 1963 – Danny Havoc and the Ventures, Chic Graham and the Coasters, Vince Earl and the Connoisseurs, The Seychelles, Wayne Gibson's Dynamic Sound and Vic and the Spidermen.

July to September 1963 – The Pathfinders, The Sabres, The Sinners, The Pawns, Bill Lesley and the Alleycats, The Exchequers, The Panthers, The Easybeats.

September 1963 – Freddie Starr and the Midnighters and The Three Spirits.

Discography Singles from 1957 to 1969

Lee Curtis and the All-stars

Little girl / Just One More Dance (Decca F 11622. 3/63)
Lets Stomp / Poor Unlucky Me (Decca F 11690. 6/63)
What About Me / I've Got My Eyes on You (Decca F 11830. 2/64)
Ecstasy / A Shot of Rhythm and Blues (Philips BF 1385. 12/64)

The Beatles

British singles on Parlophone

Love Me Do / PS, I Love You (Oct 62. R 4949)
Please Please Me / Ask Me Why (Jan 63. R 4983)
From Me to You / Thank You Girl (Apr 63. R 5015)
She Loves You / I'll Get You (Aug 63. R 5055)
I Want to Hold Your Hand / This Boy (Nov 63. R 5084)
Can't Buy Me Love / You Can't Do That (Mar 64. R 5114)
A Hard Day's Night / Thing's We Said Today (Jul 64. R 5160)
I Feel Fine / She's a Woman (Nov 64. R 5200)
Ticket to Ride / Yes It Is (Apr 65. R 5265)
Help / I'm Down (July 65. R 5305)
We Can Work it Out / Day Tripper (Dec 65. R 5389)
Paperback Writer / Rain (Jun 66. R 5452)
Eleanor Rigby / Yellow Submarine (Aug 66. R 5493)
Strawberry Fields Forever / Penny Lane (Feb 67. R 5570)
All You Need Is Love / Baby You're a Rich Man (Jul 67. R 5620)
Hello, Goodbye / I Am the Walrus (Nov 67. R 5655)
Lady Madonna / The Inner Light (Mar 68. R 5675)
Hey Jude / Revolution (Aug 68. R 5722)
Get Back / Don't Let Me Down (Apr 69. R 5777)
The Ballad of John and Yoko / Old Brown Shoe (May 69. R 5786)
Something / Come Together (Oct 69. R 5814)
Let it Be / You Know My Name (Mar 70. R 5833)

The Beatles
Decca Sessions
Audition recordings at Decca studios in London, 1 January 1962.
Like Dreamers Do, Money, Till There Was You, The Sheik of Araby, To Know Her Is to Love Her, Take Good Care of My Baby, Memphis Tennessee, Sure to Fall, Hello Little Girl, Three Cool Cats, Crying, Waiting, Hoping, Love of the Loved, September in the Rain, Besame Mucho, Searchin'.

The Big Three
Some Other Guy / Let True Love Begin (Decca F 11614. 3/63)
By the Way / Cavern Stomp (Decca F 11689. 6/63)
I'm with You / Peanut Butter (Decca F 11752. 10/63)
If You Ever Change Your Mind / You've Got to Keep Her Underhand (Decca F 11927.6/64)

The Black Knights
I Gotta Woman / Angel of Love (Columbia DB 7443. 1/65)

Bernie's Buzz Band
Don't Knock It (D Ram DM 181. 1968)
House that Jack Built (F 22829. 1968)

Chick Graham and the Coasters
Education / I Know (Decca F 11859. 2/64)
A Little You / Dance Baby, Dance (Decca F 11932. 7/64)

The Clayton Squares
Come and Get It / And Tears Fell (Decca F 12250. 10/65)

Karl Terry and the Cruisers
Haunted House / Stick it in Your Pipe (ROX OO8)

Confucius (Formerly The Hideaways)
Brandenburg Concerto / The Message (RCA 1923. 1970)

Billy J Kramer and the Dakotas
Do You Want to Know a Secret? / I'll Be on My Own (Parlophone R 5023. 4/63)
Bad to Me / I Call Your Name (Parlophone R 5049. 7/63)
I'll Keep You Satisfied / I Know (Parlophone R 5073. 10/63)

Little Children / They Remind Me of You (Parlophone R 5105. 2/64)
From a Window / Second to None (Parlophone R 5156. 7/64)
It's Gotta Last Forever / Don't Do It No More (Parlophone R 5234. 1/65)
Trains and Boats and Planes / That's the Way I Feel (Parlophone R 5285. 5/65)
Neon City / I'll Be Dog-Gone (Parlophone R 5362. 11/65)

The Dennisons
Come On Be My Girl / Little Latin Loupe Lou (Decca F 11691. 7/63)
Walkin' the Dog / You Don't Know What Love Is (Decca F 11880. 2/64)
Nobody Like My Baby / Lucy You Sure Did It This Time (Decca F 11990. 10/64)

Kingsize Taylor and the Dominoes
Memphis Tennessee / Money (Polydor NH 66990. 3/64)
Hippy Hippy Shake / Dr Feelgood (Polydor NH 66991. 3/64)
Stupidity / Bad Boy (Decca F 11874. 4/64)
Somebody's Always Trying / Looking for My Baby (Decca F 11935. 7/64)
Thinkin' / Let Me Love You (Polydor BM 56152. 65)

Lonnie Donegan
Rock Island Line / John Henry (Decca F 10647. 1955)
Diggin' My Potatoes / Take My Hand (Decca F 10695. 1956)
Lost John / Stew Ball (PYE N.15036. 1956)
Bring a Little Water, Sylvie / Dead or Alive (PYE 7N.15071. 1956)
On a Christmas Day / Take My Hand, Precious Lord (Columbia DB 3850. 1956)
Don't You Rock Me, Daddy-O / I'm Alabamy Bound (PYE N.15080. 1957)
Putting on the Style / Gamblin' Man (PYE 7N.15093. 1957)
Jack o' Diamonds / Ham 'n Eggs (PYE 7N.15116. 1957)
Cumberland Gap / Love is Strange (PYE 7N.15087. 1957)
My Dixie Darling / I'm Just a Rolling Stone (PYE 7N.15108)
The Grand Coulee Dam / Nobody Loves Like an Irishman (PYE 7N.15129. 1958)
Midnight Special / When the Sun Goes Down (PYE NJ.2006. 1958)
Sally Don't You Grieve / Betty, Betty, Betty (PYE 7N.15148. 1958)
Lonesome Traveller / Times Are Getting Hard, Boys (PYE 7N.15158. 1958)
Tom Dooley / Rock o' My Soul (PYE 7N.15172. 1958)
Does Your Chewing Gum Lose its Flavour / Aunt Rhoda (PYE 7N.15181. 1959)
Fort Worth Jail / Whoa, Buck (PYE 7N.15198. 1959)
Battle of New Orleans / Darling Corey (PYE 7N.15206. 1959)
Sal's Got a Sugar Lip / Chesapeake Bay (PYE 7N.15223. 1959)
San Miguel / Talking Guitar Blues (PYE 7N.15237. 1959)

My Old Man's a Dustman / The Golden Vanity (PYE 7N.15256. 1960)
I Wanna Go Home / Jimmy Brown the News Boy (PYE 7N.15267. 1960)
Lorelei / In All My Wildest Dreams (PYE 7N.15275. 1960)
Lively / Black Cat (PYE 7N.15312. 1960)
Virgin Mary / Beyond the Sunset (PYE 7N.15315. 1960)
Bury Me Beneath the Willow / Leave My Woman Alone (PYE 7N.15330. 1961)
Have a Drink on Me / Seven Golden Daffodils (PYE 7N.15355. 1961)
Michael Row the Boat Ashore / Lumbered (PYE 7N.15371. 1961)
The Comancheros / Ramblin' Round (PYE 7N.15410. 1961)
The Party's Over / Over the Rainbow (PYE 7N.15424. 1962)
I'll Never Fall in Love Again / Keep on the Sunny Side (PYE 7N.15446. 1962)
Pick a Bale of Cotton / Steal Away (PYE 7N.15455. 1962)
Lonnie also recorded EPs and LPs during his playing career.

The Escorts

Dizzy Miss Lizzy / All I Want Is You (Fontana TF 453. 4/64)
The One to Cry / Tell Me, Baby (Fontana TF 474. 6/64)
I Don't Want to Go on Without You / Don't Forget to Write (Fontana TF 516. 11/64)
Come Home, Baby / You'll Get No Lovin' That Way (Fontana TF 570. 5/65)
From Head to Toe / Night Time (Columbia DB 8061. 1966)

Faron's Flamingos

Do You Love Me / See if She Cares (Oriole CB 1834. 8/63)
Shake Sherry / Give Me Time (Oriole CB 1867. 10/63)

The Fourmost

Hello Little Girl / Just in Case (Parlophone R 5056. 9/63)
I'm in Love / Respectable (Parlophone R 5078. 12/63)
A Little Loving / Waiting for You (Parlophone R 5128. 4/64)
How Can I Tell Her / You've Got That Way (Parlophone R 5157. 7/64)
Baby I Need Your Loving / That's Only What They Say (Parlophone R 5194. 11/64)
Everything in the Garden / He Could Never (Parlophone R 5304. 7/65)
Girls, Girls, Girls / Why Do Fools Fall in Love? (Parlophone R 5379. 11/65)

The Harlems

It Takes a Fool Like Me (Dick James Music)

Rory Storm and the Hurricanes

Dr Feelgood / I Can Tell (Oriole CB 1858. 12/64)

America / Since You Broke My Heart (Parlophone R 5197. 11/64)

The Liverpool Scene

The Woo-Woo / Love Is (RCA 1816. 69)

The Merseys

Sorrow / Some Other Day (Fontana TF 694. 66)

The Cat / Change of Heart (Fontana TF 845. 67)

Penny in My Pocket / I Hope You're Happy (Fontana TF 916. 68)

The Merseybeats

Its Love That Really Counts / The Fortune-Teller (Fontana TF 412. 8/63)

I Think of You / Mister Moonlight (Fontana TF 431. 1/64)

Don't Turn Around / Really Mystified (Fontana TF 459. 4/64)

Wishin' and Hopin' / Milkman (Fontana TF 482. 6/64)

Last Night / See Me Back (Fontana TF 10/64)

Don't Let it Happen to Us / It Would Take a Long Time (Fontana TF 568. 5/65)

I Love You, Yes I Do / Good, Good Lovin' (Fontana TF 507. 9/65)

I Stand Accused / All My Life (Fontana TF 645. 12/65)

Freddie Starr and the Midnighters

Who Told You / Peter Gunn (Decca F11 663. 5/63)

Baby Blue / It's Shaking Time (Decca F11 786. 11/64)

Never Cry on Someone's Shoulder / Keep on Dreaming (Decca F1 2009. 9/64)

Gerry and the Pacemakers

How Do You Do It / Away From You (Columbia DB 4987. 14/3/63)

I Like It / It's Happened to Me (Columbia DB 7041. 5/630)

You'll Never Walk Alone / It's Alright (DB 7126. 10/10/63)

I'm the One / You've Got What I Like (Columbia DB 7189)

Don't Let the Sun Catch You Crying / Show Me That You Care (Columbia DB 7268)

Its Gonna be Alright / It's Just Because (Columbia DB 7357. 3/9/64)

Ferry 'Cross the Mersey / You, You, You (Columbia DB 7437. 17/12/64)

I'll Be There / Baby You're So Good to Me (Columbia DB 7504. 25/3/65)

Walk Hand in Hand / Dreams (Columbia DB 7738. 18/11/65)

Girl on a Swing / Fool to Me (Columbia DB 8044. 66)

The Quarry Men

(Recording at Philips Studio in Kensington, Liverpool.)

That'll be the Day / In Spite of All the Danger

The Remo Four

I Wish I Could Shimmy Like My Sister Kate / Peter Gunn (Piccadilly 7 N.3517. 4/64)
Sally Go Round the Roses / I Know a Girl (Piccadilly 7 N.35186. 6/64)

Denny Seyton and the Sabres

Tricky Dicky / Baby What You Want Me to Do (Mercury MF 800. 2/64)
Short Fat Fanny / Give Me Back My Heart (Mercury MF 814. 6/64)
The Way You Look Tonight / Hands Off (Mercury MF 824. 9/64)

The Searchers

Sweet's for My Sweet / It's Been a Dream (PYE 7N.15533. 27/6/63)
Sweet Nothin's / What'd I Say (Philips BF 1274. 10/10/63)
Sugar and Spice / Saints (PYE 7N.15566. 24/10/63)
Needles and Pins / Saturday Night Out (PYE 7N.15594. 1/64)
Don't Throw Your Love Away / I Pretend I'm with You (PYE 7N.15630. 16/4/64)
Someday We're Gonna Love Again / No One Else Could Love You (PYE 7N.156701.6/7/64)
When You Walk in the Room / I'll Be Missing You (PYE 7N.15694. 17/9/64)
What Have They Done to the Rain / This Feeling Inside (PYE 7N.15739. 3/12/64)
Goodbye, My Love / Till I Meet You (PYE 7N.15794. 4/3/65)
He's Got No Love / So Far Away (PYE 7N.15878. 8/7/65)
When I Get Home / I'm Never Coming Back (PYE 7N.15905. 14/10/65)
Take Me for What I'm Worth / Too Many Miles (PYE 7N.15992. 11/12/65)
Take It, or Leave It / Don't Hide It Away (PYE 7N.17094. 21/4/66)
Have You Ever Loved Somebody / It's Just the Way (PYE 7N.17170. 13/10/66)

The Swinging Blue Jeans

It's Too Late Now / Think of Me (HMV POP 1170. 6/63)
Do You Know / Angie (HMV POP 1206. 9/63)
Hippy Hippy Shake / Know I Must Go (HMV POP 1242. 12/63)
Good Golly Miss Molly / Shakin' Feelin' (HMV POP 1273. 3/64)
You're No Good / Don't You Worry About Me (HMV POP 1304. 5/64)
Promise You'll Tell Her / It's Alright (HMV POP 1327. 8/64)
It Isn't There / One of These Days (HMV POP 1375. 12/64)
Make Me Know / I've Got a Girl (HMV POP 1409. 3/65)
Crazy 'Bout My Baby / Good Lovin' (HMV POP 1477. 10/65)

The Takers

If You Don't Come Back / Think (PYE 7N.15690. 9/64)

The Undertakers

Everybody Loves a Lover / Mashed Potatoes (PYE 7N.15543.7/63)
What About Us / Money (PYE 7N.15562.10/63)
Just a Little Bit / Stupidity (PYE 7N.15607. 2/64)

Ian and the Zodiacs

Beechwood 4.5789 / You Can Think Again (Oriole CB 1849. 1963)
Just the Little Thing / This Won't Happen to Me (Fontana TF 548. 1965)

Discography of Albums from 1957 to 1969

The Beatles up to 1969

Please Please Me (Parlophone PMC 1202. 1963)
With The Beatles (Parlophone PMC 1206. 1963)
A Hard Day's Night (Parlophone PMC 1230. 1964)
Beatles For Sale (Parlophone PMC 1240. 1964)
Help (Parlophone PMC 1255. 1965)
Rubber Soul (Parlophone PMC 1267. 1965)
Revolver (Parlophone PMC 7009. 1966)
Sergeant Pepper (Parlophone PCS 7027. 1967)
The Beatles (Apple PCS 7167. 1968)
Yellow Submarine (Apple PCS 7070. 1969)
Abbey Road (Apple PCS 7088. 1969)

The Fourmost

First and Fourmost (Parlophone PMC 1259. 1965)

Billy Fury to 1969

The Sound of Fury (Decca LF 1329. 1960)
Half Way to Paradise (Ace of Clubs 1083. 1961)
Billy (Decca LK 4533. 1963)
We Want Billy (Decca LK 4548. 1963)

Billy J Kramer to 1969

Listen (Parlophone (PMC 1209. 1963)
Billy Boy (MFP 1134. 1966)
Little Children (Imperial LP 9267)
I'll Keep You Satisfied (Imperial LP 12273)
Trains and Boats and Planes (Imperial LP 929)

The Liverpool Scene

The Incredible Adventures (RCA Sep 1968)
Bread on the Night (RCA June 1969)

The Merseybeats to 1969

The Merseybeats (Fontana TL 5210. 1964)

Gerry and the Pacemakers

How Do You Like It? (Columbia 33 SX 1546. 10/63) No 2 for 28 weeks.
Ferry cross the Mersey (Columbia 33 SX 1676) No 19 1 week.
You'll Never Walk Alone (MFP 1101. 1966)

Denny Seyton and the Sabres

It's the Gear (Wing WL 1032. 1965)

The Searchers

Meet the Searchers (PYE NPL 18086. 7/63)
Sugar and Spice (PYE NPL 18089. 11/63)
It's the Searchers (PYE NPL 18092. 5/64)
Sounds Like the Searchers (PYE 18111. 3/65)
Take Me for What I'm Worth (PYE NPL 18120. 12/65)
The Searchers' Smash Hits (Marble Arch MAL 640. 1966)
The Searchers Smash Hits (Vol 2 Marble Arch MAL 673. 1967)

Swinging Blue Jeans

Blue Jeans a Swinging (HMV 1802. 1964)

Ian and the Zodiacs

Gear Again (Wing WL 1074. 1965)

There were many singles, EPs and albums that were produced for export to places like America and Europe, but I have just given you a sample of some of the UK releases. I have also included just a few of the groups who made their contribution to the Merseybeat boom which, by 1965, was almost over. For myself, it was groups like The Remo Four, The Big Three, The Undertakers, Rory Storm and the Hurricanes, The Beatles, Faron's Flamingos and The Swinging Blue Jeans, who made the most memorable marks.

Some of Liverpool's Promoters

It was the promoters who had the foresight to recognise the potential of some of the venues around Liverpool, which enabled the Merseybeat groups to develop their unique sounds.

Allan Williams was a promoter and also a club and coffee bar owner. He was the man behind The Beatles' first Hamburg booking, although other people in the business didn't have the same opinion about The Silver Beetles, as they were then known. Allan recognised their talent and potential and his faith in them paid off. Prior to this, Jacaranda Enterprise booked the Liverpool Stadium in conjunction with Larry Parnes – a well-established London promoter – featuring American stars Eddie Cochran and Gene Vincent, who had previously appeared at the Liverpool Empire for Parnes. While ticket sales were booming, news came through that Eddie Cochran had been killed in a car crash in Wiltshire on 17 April 1960. Gene Vincent still honoured the booking in memory of his great friend. The Silver Beetles made a lasting impression on Allan Williams and he also started booking some of Liverpool's up and coming groups like Rory Storm and the Hurricanes, Gerry and the Pacemakers, as well as Cass and the Casanovas, who later changed their name to The Big Three.
Sam Leach also played a major role in the Merseybeat revolution, by

PERKINS SPORTS ASSOCIATION
MIDSUMMER
BEAT CARNIVAL
SATURDAY, 20th JUNE on the SPORTS GROUND
IN GIANT MARQUEES with SPECIAL FLOORING
7.30 p.m. — midnight
KENNY LYNCH
Star of Radio and T.V.
and
THE LAURIE JAY COMBO
and 3 MERSEYSIDE GROUPS
THE 4 TUNES
THE KRUZADES
THE CROUPIERS
and
THE
Arthur Howes presents
The Billy J. Kramer Show
starring
Billy J. Kramer and the Dakotas
Tommy Roe
Heinz and the Saints
The Dennisons ★ The Fourmost
Johnny Sandon and the Remo Four
Tommy Quickly ★ Chris Carlsen

promoting headlining shows at venues like the Tower Ballroom, New Brighton, featuring Emile Ford and the Checkmates with supporting acts such as The Beatles, Gerry and the Pacemakers, Howie Casey and the Seniors, Rory Storm and the Hurricanes and The Big Three. What an amazing line-up of top Liverpool groups for just six shillings! He also used the Jazz Society Club at Number 13 Temple Street, which most people will remember as the Iron Door Club. He introduced all-night Rock and Roll, featuring twelve of the most talented groups from Merseyside: Gerry and the Pacemakers, The Beatles, The Remo Four, Rory Storm and the Hurricanes, Kingsize Taylor and the Dominoes, The Big Three, Dale Roberts and the Jaywalkers, Derry and the Seniors, Ray and the Del-Renas, The Pressmen, Johnny Rocco and the Jets, and Faron and the Tempest Tornadoes.

Bob Wooler was also involved in promoting shows and he too used the Tower Ballroom, New Brighton, in conjunction with Brian Epstein, who valued his vast knowledge of local talent. On one of his shows he had top Rock and Roll star, Little Richard, with support acts The Beatles, The Big Three, Lee Curtis and the All Stars, Billy Kramer and the Coasters, Pete McClain and the Dakotas, Rory Storm and the Hurricanes, The Undertakers, The Four Jays, The Merseybeats and Gus Travis and the Midnighters. Bob was involved in quite a number of these shows.

I think most people will also remember him as a DJ at the Cavern and he was involved in some of the riverboat cruises on board the *Royal Iris*, featuring some of the Cavern's regular groups – The Clayton Squares, The Hideaways, Earl Preston and the Realms, St Louis Checks, The Roadrunners, The Richmond Group, Amos Bony and the TTs, plus guest artists, The Measles. Bob was not only extremely likeable, he was also quite a pragmatic promoter. During a conversation with him I asked who he thought should have made it, apart from The Beatles and his answer was Earl Preston and TTs.

Charlie McBain was one of Liverpool's early promoters operating in the 1950s and 1960s, booking such groups as The Quarry Men, The Blue Genes, Rory Storm's Skiffle Group and The Raving Texans. He would use venues such as Wilson Hall, in Garston and Holyoake Hall, on Smithdown Road, which became quite a well known dance venue for many of Liverpool's up and coming groups. Garston Swimming Baths was another of his venues but became quite notorious because of the frequent fights that broke out there. He would also book groups for the Town Hall, Wavertree and the Conservative Club in Norris Green.

Brian Kelly went under the name of Bee-Kay Promotions. His major venues were halls such as Litherland Town Hall, which was an impressive dance hall and featured some of Merseyside's foremost groups, including Kingsize Taylor and the Dominoes, The Beatles and Gerry and the Pacemakers. Another Brian Kelly venue was the Aintree Institute on Longmoor Lane. The Beatles frequently performed at this club, along with people such as Faron's Flamingos and The Merseybeats. The Alexandra Hall, Crosby, also held Bee-Kay promotion nights. The list goes on.

Wally Hill was another of Merseyside's promoters and organised dances at Blair Hall, Walton. Despite its humble situation over the Co-op, many of the top groups played at this venue. Wally also used the David Lewis Theatre, in Liverpool and Holyoake Hall, Wavertree.

Jim Gretty There were numerous other promoters and managers in Liverpool, but there is one person I could not leave out – that well known character, Jim Gretty. As many of the Liverpool musicians who used to visit Frank Hessy's music shop, where he worked as a salesman, will know, Jim also had a long-standing background in the business as a performer, as well as being a promoter. I found him to be someone who had time for everyone and I suppose most of the musicians will have their own memories of him. Whenever he showed you a new guitar or amplifier that had just come into the shop, he would be more than happy to demonstrate it for you, but always seemed to play the same song – *Freight Train*. Sad to say, Jim is no longer with us, but all the musicians that knew him will have very fond memories of him.

On 15 October 1961, Jim, in conjunction with George Martin, put on a charity show in aid of St John's Ambulance Brigade, which was held at the Albany Cinema in Maghull. Top of the bill was Ken Dodd, supported by The Dusty Road Ramblers, Les Arnold, Joe Cordover, Dunn and Markey, Bob McGrady, Lennie Rens, Shirley Gordon, Bert King, The Eltones, The Beatles, Denis Horton and Gladys Ambrose, Jackie Owen and the Joe Royal Trio, Edna Bell, Jim Gretty and Dennis Smerdon. The compere for the show was Arthur Scott.

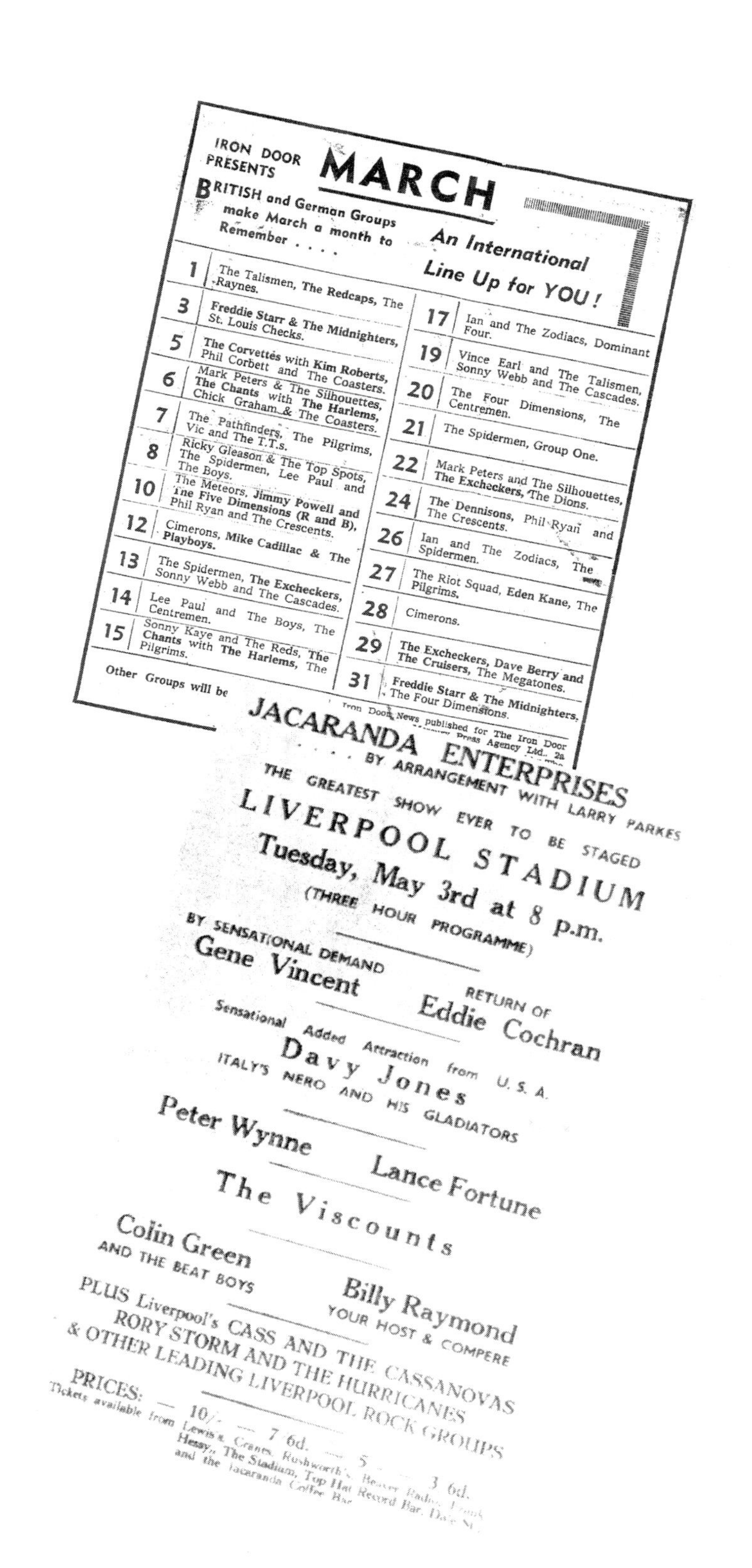
IRON DOOR PRESENTS
MARCH
BRITISH and German Groups make March a month to Remember . . . .
An International Line Up for YOU!

1	The Talismen, The Redcaps, The Raynes.
3	**Freddie Starr & The Midnighters,** St. Louis Checks.
5	**The Corvettes** with **Kim Roberts,** Phil Corbett and The Coasters.
6	Mark Peters & The Silhouettes, **The Chants** with **The Harlems,** Chick Graham & The Coasters.
7	The Pathfinders, The Pilgrims, Vic and The T.T.s.
8	Ricky Gleason & The Top Spots, The Spidermen, Lee Paul and The Boys.
10	The Meteors, **Jimmy Powell and The Five Dimensions (R and B),** Phil Ryan and The Crescents.
12	Cimerons, **Mike Cadillac & The Playboys.**
13	The Spidermen, **The Exchecker**s, Sonny Webb and The Cascades.
14	Lee Paul and The Boys, The Centremen.
15	Sonny Kaye and The Reds, **The Chants** with **The Harlems,** The Pilgrims.
17	Ian and The Zodiacs, Dominant Four.
19	Vince Earl and The Talismen, Sonny Webb and The Cascades.
20	The Four Dimensions, The Centremen.
21	The Spidermen, Group One.
22	Mark Peters and The Silhouettes, **The Excheckers,** The Dions.
24	**The Dennisons,** Phil Ryan and The Crescents.
26	Ian and The Zodiacs, The Spidermen.
27	The Riot Squad, **Eden Kane,** The Pilgrims.
28	Cimerons.
29	**The Excheckers, Dave Berry and The Cruisers,** The Megatones.
31	**Freddie Starr & The Midnighters,** The Four Dimensions.

Other Groups will be

Iron Door News published for The Iron Door ... Press Agency Ltd., 2a

JACARANDA ENTERPRISES
. . . BY ARRANGEMENT WITH LARRY PARKES
THE GREATEST SHOW EVER TO BE STAGED
LIVERPOOL STADIUM
Tuesday, May 3rd at 8 p.m.
(THREE HOUR PROGRAMME)
BY SENSATIONAL DEMAND
Gene Vincent
RETURN OF
Eddie Cochran
Sensational Added Attraction from U.S.A.
Davy Jones
ITALY'S NERO AND HIS GLADIATORS
Peter Wynne
Lance Fortune
The Viscounts
Colin Green
AND THE BEAT BOYS
Billy Raymond
YOUR HOST & COMPERE
PLUS Liverpool's CASS AND THE CASSANOVAS
RORY STORM AND THE HURRICANES
& OTHER LEADING LIVERPOOL ROCK GROUPS
PRICES: — 10/- — 7/6d. — 5/- — 3/6d.
Tickets available from Lewis's, Cranes, Rushworth's, Beaver Radio, Frank Hessy, The Stadium, Top Hat Record Bar, Dale St. and the Jacaranda Coffee Bar

Dave Forshaw, Promoter

The Beechwoods.

Dave Forshaw played a major role in promoting local groups, including two of which I was a member in the sixties. St Luke's Club, in Crosby is one venue, in particular that springs to mind whenever Dave's name is mentioned. Dave was also involved in sending groups over to Hamburg, as were many of the other local promoters. I think Dave must have been one of the youngest amongst them, yet he booked groups like The Searchers and The Beatles at local clubs, groups that became household names. He is still involved in the Merseybeat era as a member of The Merseycats children's charity, raising money for the children of Merseyside.

Below, I have picked just a handful of groups that came out of Merseyside and were on Dave's books in the early 1960s. As you can see, my objective was to mention some of the groups that were overshadowed by the better known groups, such as The Beatles. Liverpool and Wallasey produced literally hundreds of extraordinarily good groups who never received any recognition. Not all of these were Merseybeat groups, some played Soul and some Country, Jazz or Skiffle, but they all had an influence on the developments in music in the 1960s.

Danny and the Asteroids
The Beechwoods
The Bellboys
The Bentics
The Blue Set
The Bobcats
The Beatles
Beckets Kim
Frank Knight and the Barons
The Casuals
The Calderstones
The Capitals
Cy Tucker and the Cimarrons
The Classics
The Comancheros
The Commotions
The Connoisseurs
The Denims
Dex Dooley
The Dennisons
The Del Renas
The Dixieland Jazz Band
The Pontiacs
The Pitiful
The Rig
The Ravens
Clay Ellis and the Raiders
The Searchers
The Seftons
The Shades
The Small Unit
The Sorrels
Vic and the Spidermen
Adam and the Sinners
The Silver Tones
The Silhouettes
Vince Wade and the Statesmen
The Democrats
Steve Day and the Drifters
The Flintstones
The Five Shillings
Force One
The Falcons
The Four Clefs
The Four Jays
The Galvanisers
The Hi-Cats
The Invaders
Johnny and the Jets
Joe Rutherford Jazz Band
Karl Terry
The Lee Eddie Five
The Magnolia Jazz Band
The Mavericks
Tommy Lowe and the Metronomes
The Mustangs
The Night Boppers
The Onlookers
The Pressmen
The Strangers
The Sundowners
The Syndicate
The Talismen
Gus and the Thundercaps
The Toreadors
Tomorrow's People
The Tropic
Earl Preston's TTs
The Twig
Tyme and Motion
The Valiants
The Vince Diamond Trio
The Volcanoes
The Zeros